PROFICIENCY-BASED
INSTRUCTION

rethinking lesson design and delivery

Property Of
Jeffry B. Fuller

eric   mark   anthony r.   troy

TWADELL   **ONUSCHECK**   **REIBEL**   **GOBBLE**

Solution Tree | Press

a division of
Solution Tree

555 North Morton Street
Bloomington, IN 47404
800.733.6786 (toll free) / 812.336.7700
FAX: 812.336.7790

email: info@SolutionTree.com
SolutionTree.com

Visit **go.SolutionTree.com/instruction** to download the free reproducibles in this book.

Printed in the United States of America

Library of Congress Cataloging-in-Publication Data

Names: Twadell, Eric, author.
Title: Proficiency-based instruction : rethinking lesson design and delivery
  / Eric Twadell, Mark Onuscheck, Anthony R. Reibel, and Troy Gobble.
Description: Bloomington, Indiana : Solution Tree Press, [2019] | Includes
  bibliographical references and index.
Identifiers: LCCN 2018050760 | ISBN 9781947604179 (perfect bound)
Subjects: LCSH: Competency-based education.
Classification: LCC LC1031 .T93 2019 | DDC 371.3028--dc23 LC record available at
https://lccn.loc.gov/2018050760

Solution Tree

Jeffrey C. Jones, CEO
Edmund M. Ackerman, President

Solution Tree Press

President and Publisher: Douglas M. Rife
Associate Publisher: Sarah Payne-Mills
Art Director: Rian Anderson
Managing Production Editor: Kendra Slayton
Senior Production Editor: Christine Hood
Content Development Specialist: Amy Rubenstein
Copy Editor: Miranda Addonizio
Proofreader: Sarah Ludwig
Text and Cover Designer: Rian Anderson
Editorial Assistant: Sarah Ludwig

The authors intend to donate all of their royalties to the Stevenson High School Foundation.

Dedication

To the faculty and staff of Adlai E. Stevenson High School. We stand in awe of your relentless pursuit of our mission of *Success for Every Student*.

Acknowledgments

As friends and colleagues, we often find ourselves expressing how grateful we are to work at Adlai E. Stevenson High School in Lincolnshire, Illinois. While others refer to Stevenson as "the birthplace of the PLC movement," we simply refer to it as home. We are blessed to work with an administrative team that is constantly looking to improve our collective work and a board of education that includes: Steve Frost, Dave Weisberg, Terry Moons, Gary Gorson, Sunit Jain, Heena Agrawal, and Amy Neault. These remarkable leaders continue to hold us all to high expectations and push us toward our mission of *Success for Every Student*. They demand that we should want for all students what we would want for our own students. It is our absolute privilege to serve a community and board of education that puts students and their learning at the heart of their decision making.

While we certainly have some responsibility for leading this new model of proficiency-based instruction, none of it would be possible without the hard work and amazing dedication of the faculty of Adlai E. Stevenson High School. We continue to stand in awe of our teachers' dedication to students and their constant search for new ways to improve their professional practice. The cycle of continuous improvement is deeply embedded in the culture of teaching and learning among our faculty, and we are proud to serve as their storytellers.

We are grateful for our friends at Solution Tree who continue to believe in us and the work that we are doing. Jeff Jones, Ed Ackerman, and Douglas Rife have been supportive in our efforts to continue to share the amazing work that is happening at Adlai E. Stevenson High School. We have made new friends in the Press division, including Amy Rubenstein and Christine Hood, who have helped shape our ideas and improve our writing. And, we are especially grateful for the friendships that we continue to have with Shannon

Ritz, Macy Hughes, Anna Hazinski, Ali Cummins, and the rest of their team, as they have all been supportive in our efforts to share many stories of the amazing work that is happening in our school and consortium.

Solution Tree Press would like to thank the following reviewers:

Melody Apezteguia
Assistant Principal
American Fork High School
American Fork, Utah

Dustin Barrett
Principal
Meridian Academy
Meridian, Idaho

Paul Cone Jr.
Middle School Principal
Canisteo-Greenwood Central School
Canisteo, New York

Candace Jay
English Teacher
Fruita Middle School
Fruita, Colorado

Brig Leane
PLC Associate
Grand Junction, Colorado

Ryan Rydstrom
Associate Director of Access and
    Instructional Design
Cedar Rapids Community School
    District
Cedar Rapids, Iowa

Kim Zeydel
Math Teacher
Meridian Academy
Meridian, Idaho

Visit **go.SolutionTree.com/instruction** to download the free reproducibles in this book.

Table of Contents

Reproducibles are in italics.

About the Authors

Eric Twadell, PhD, is superintendent of Adlai E. Stevenson High School in Lincolnshire, Illinois. He has been a social studies teacher, curriculum director, and assistant superintendent for leadership and organizational development.

Stevenson High School has been described by the United States Department of Education (USDE) as one of the most recognized and celebrated schools in America and is one of only three schools to win the USDE National Blue Ribbon Schools award on four occasions. Stevenson was one of the first comprehensive schools designated a New American High School by USDE as a model of successful school reform and is repeatedly cited as one of America's top high schools and the "birthplace" of the Professional Learning Communities at Work® (PLC) process.

Eric is a coauthor who has also written several professional articles. As a dedicated PLC practitioner, he has worked with state departments of education and local schools and districts nationwide to achieve school improvement and reform. An accessible and articulate authority on PLC concepts, Eric brings hands-on experience to his presentations and workshops.

In addition to his teaching and leadership roles, Eric has been involved in coaching numerous athletic teams and facilitating outdoor education and adventure travel programs. He is a member of many professional organizations.

Eric earned a master's degree in curriculum and instruction and a doctorate in educational leadership and policies studies from Loyola University Chicago.

To learn more about Eric's work, follow him @ELT247365 on Twitter.

Mark Onuscheck is director of curriculum, instruction, and assessment at Adlai E. Stevenson High School in Lincolnshire, Illinois. He is a former English teacher and director of communication arts. As director of curriculum, instruction, and assessment, Mark works with academic divisions around professional learning, articulation, curricular and instructional revision, evaluation, assessment, social emotional learning, technologies, and Common Core implementation. He is also an adjunct professor at DePaul University.

Mark was awarded the Quality Matters Star Rating for his work in online teaching. He helps to build curriculum and instructional practices for TimeLine Theatre's arts integration program for Chicago Public Schools. Additionally, he is a National Endowment for the Humanities' grant recipient and a member of the Association for Supervision and Curriculum Development, National Council of Teachers of English, International Literacy Association, and Learning Forward.

Mark earned a bachelor's degree in English and classical studies from Allegheny College and a master's degree in teaching English from the University of Pittsburgh.

Anthony R. Reibel is director of assessment, research, and evaluation at Adlai E. Stevenson High School in Illinois. He administers assessments, manages student achievement data, and oversees instructional practice. Anthony began his professional career as a technology specialist and entrepreneur. After managing several businesses, he became a Spanish teacher at Stevenson. He has also served as a curricular team leader, core team leader, coach, and club sponsor.

In 2010, Anthony received recognition from the state of Illinois, and in 2011, the Illinois Computing Educators named him Technology Educator of the Year. He is a member of the Association for Supervision and Curriculum Development, Illinois Principals Association, Illinois Computing Educators, and American Council on the Teaching of Foreign Languages.

He earned a bachelor's degree in Spanish from Indiana University and master's degrees (one in curriculum and instruction and a second in educational leadership) from Roosevelt University.

To learn more about Anthony's work, follow him @areibel on Twitter.

Troy Gobble is principal of Adlai E. Stevenson High School in Lincolnshire, Illinois. He previously served as assistant principal for teaching and learning at Stevenson. Troy taught science for eighteen years and served as the science department chair for eight years at Riverside Brookfield High School in Riverside, Illinois.

The USDE describes Stevenson as "the most recognized and celebrated school in America," and Stevenson is one of only three schools to win the USDE National Blue Ribbon Schools award on four occasions. Stevenson was one of the first comprehensive schools that the USDE designated a New American High School as a model of successful school reform, and it is repeatedly cited as one of America's top high schools and the birthplace of the PLC at Work process.

Troy holds a master of science in educational administration from Benedictine University, a master of science in natural sciences (physics) from Eastern Illinois University, and a bachelor's degree in secondary science education from the University of Illinois at Urbana-Champaign.

To book Eric Twadell, Mark Onuscheck, Anthony R. Reibel, or Troy Gobble for professional development, contact pd@SolutionTree.com.

Introduction

Teaching likes order. But as it turns out, learning doesn't.

For decades, educators have committed to an orderly, planned, sequential, linear, and time-bound approach to teaching and learning. We see these traditional values manifested in many different ways in our teaching practices and the ways in which we organize schools—from how we arrange classrooms in rows, to bell schedules, to the thousands of different curriculum guides arranged as if learning results from a step-by-step instructional recipe. Education operates in an assembly-line mindset, where schools place students on a conveyor belt in kindergarten until they are fully manufactured and ready to graduate from high school.

In this book, and in our other books, we confront this mindset and reinvent conversations about teaching and learning that focus on the proficiency development of every student—recognizing that every student is different and that they all learn at different rates, at different times, and in different ways. In this book, we want to reinvent the way schools consider the basics of lesson planning and delivery so that developing the proficiency of every learner is built into the format of every lesson. In doing so, we believe teaching and learning practices can better address the needs of every learner in an immediate, highly responsive way.

Of course, on some level, we recognize that valuing order and efficiency makes sense in a number of school decisions; however, we cannot achieve success for every student by herding students through classrooms at the same pace, in the same way, at the same time. This traditional process appears to work for some students, but a one-size-fits-all approach to teaching and learning is a deeply flawed notion. Unfortunately, this approach has been the longstanding format for lesson design and delivery.

To change how we think about lesson planning, we call into question how traditional approaches to teaching and learning limit the success of every student and guide a discussion that promotes teaching and learning practices that support the capacity, proficiency, and mastery of every student—practices that require a nonstop commitment to success for *every student.*

In our two previous books, *Proficiency-Based Assessment: Process, Not Product* (Gobble, Onuscheck, Reibel, & Twadell, 2016) and *Pathways to Proficiency: Implementing Evidence-Based Grading* (Gobble, Onuscheck, Reibel, & Twadell, 2017), we lead discussions that support major shifts in thinking about teaching and learning. In these two books, we discuss the importance of supporting the proficiency of every student through how we assess students, grade students, and report on student growth. In this book, we want to tackle how we can better approach *instruction.* To improve on past instructional practices, we know that we must examine more closely how developing student proficiency requires a departure from traditionally structured lesson planning.

Here, we address our concerns about traditional approaches to instructional practices by taking a hard look at the way we build lesson plans. We assert that lesson plans should focus on developing proficiency in students, which means abandoning the traditional one-size-fits-all approach to traditional lesson planning.

We recognize that assembly lines work well for building cars and toys, but the orderly, planned, sequential, linear, and time-bound method of the assembly line doesn't work for learning. Learning is messy, spontaneous, irregular, nonlinear, and asynchronous. Knowing that these variables are always at play, we need to reassess our assumptions of teaching and re-approach our educational choices. To do this, we must plan with the learner in mind, which means embracing what we know about how learning really works. As we consider building lessons, planning with the learner in mind is essential and requires upending decades of assumptions, as shown in table I.1.

Table I.1: Assumptions for Teaching and Realities of Learning

Assumptions for Teaching	Realities of Learning
Orderly	Messy
Planned	Spontaneous
Sequential	Irregular
Linear	Nonlinear
Time bound	Asynchronous

Traditional lesson-planning structures reflect these longstanding assumptions. The habits of traditional lesson planning follow our assumptions for teaching and ignore what we know about learning. Traditional lesson plans approach teaching as if it can be and should be the following.

- ▶ **Orderly:** We assume that all learners benefit from the same arrangements of activities during a lesson and that that order benefits all learners no matter their ability or skill.

- ▶ **Planned:** We assume that we can prepare all class lesson plans far in advance of knowing what our students know and what they don't know. Likewise, we can use these plans year after year, assuming learners are the same year after year.

- ▶ **Sequential:** We assume that if we sequence lessons into units, we can create the magical, sequenced combination that ensures all students learn the material by the end of the unit.

- ▶ **Linear:** We assume learning is a linear experience for all students, and the teacher's job is to move students from point A to point B during a lesson.

- ▶ **Time bound:** We assume learning follows a time line and students learn according to the time a teacher commits to a lesson or unit. We assume that it is acceptable to move onward even if all students are not demonstrating proficiency.

Our concern with the structure of traditional lesson planning is that it ignores what we know about the learning process. The learning process works in opposition to our assumptions for teaching. We need to consider our lessons with the realities of learning in mind. The reality of learning is that it is often:

- ▶ **Messy**—Students' concentration fades in and out during a lesson—some miss a step in the order, some can't or won't follow along, and some already know the material and are bored. Some students make mistakes, and they might learn but need to relearn.

- ▶ **Spontaneous**—Learning doesn't just happen because we want it to and when we want it to. Learning often happens in organic, unexpected ways, at unexpected times.

- ▶ **Irregular**—There is no one lesson design and delivery model that is going to be suitable for every learner.

▸ **Nonlinear**—When we think of learning as moving students from point A to point B, we overlook the fact that there are gaps in learning for many students.

▸ **Asynchronous**—Learning and student growth cannot be tied to the calendar or the clock. We need to better address and support learning that is happening beyond arbitrary deadlines. Learning happens at different rates and different paces.

In many cases, our traditional assumptions about teaching continue to govern the classroom and how teachers plan lessons. These deeply rooted assumptions are ingrained in the way we structure lessons. The most regarded lesson-planning models come from the time-honored suggestions of experts like Madeline Hunter (1982), who promoted lesson templates that presume learning is an ordered, planned, sequential, linear, and time-bound experience for students. Hunter's (1982) work *Mastery Teaching: Increasing Instructional Effectiveness in Elementary and Secondary Schools, Colleges, and Universities* unpacks what "good" lessons should include. Within these templates, teachers build lesson plans in parts, assuming that all students begin at the same place in their learning and hoping they also end up in the same place. We want to challenge the ways those components are built, paying close attention to whether they have been oversimplified and, perhaps, misinterpreted.

Examining the Hunter Lesson-Planning Model

The Hunter lesson-planning model is familiar to most teachers; in fact, most can probably recite it by heart. Outlined in Hunter's (1982) book *Mastery Teaching*, the Hunter lesson-planning template comprises seven parts.

1. **The lesson begins with an *anticipatory set*:** This usually refers to previous learning or prior knowledge, or it works to engage students.

2. **The lesson states the lesson's objectives or purpose:** The teacher communicates the expectations for student learning. Again, this comes at the beginning of the lesson.

3. **The lesson provides instructional input:** At this point in the lesson, the teacher presents or tells students the new knowledge they are expected to learn that day.

4. **The teacher models the new learning or objective:** In the modeling portion of the lesson, the teacher demonstrates any new skill

so students can see an example of how to perform the objective or how to incorporate the new knowledge learned through instructional input.

5. **The teacher checks for understanding to make sure all students comprehend the instructional input:** The teacher checks how well students understand what was modeled and the new learning. He or she might do this through questioning strategies.

6. **The lesson allows for guided practice:** During this time, students engage in an activity to practice the objective and the new learning, and the teacher answers questions to ensure students grasp the new material.

7. **The teacher gives students opportunities for independent practice:** By the end of the lesson and through guided practice, students are expected to perform the skills on their own. The teacher then assigns homework that allows students to practice without needing supervision.

We argue that we should consider the seven stages of a lesson more deeply, focusing more intentionally on students' developing proficiency. As we outline in this book, the goal in each lesson is for the teacher to become more attentive to each learner's development. Better lesson plans are focused on growth.

Not surprisingly, the traditional model of lesson planning has given rise to a number of instructional delivery methods tied to misguided assumptions that are not firmly committed to developing expectations for proficiency. We should reconsider the following instructional delivery methods, which have become habits in teaching and learning.

▸ Separate and rigid

▸ Passive engagement

▸ Short-term application and shallow recall

▸ Time bound

▸ Teacher centered

▸ Based on gradual release of responsibility model

Separate and Rigid

We can sum up current instructional practices with the idea of scaffolding. We believe that the problem with scaffolding is that it moves from simple to more complex with the assumption that at each step, students are 100 percent successful. It's for this very reason that students do not see any need to reflect or consider continuous improvement—because they are always successful. This separate and rigid nature to learning produces overconfident learners and isolationist thinkers. By seeing each part as separate, the learner can lose connectedness to the whole.

Passive Engagement

The linear nature of scaffolding then breeds what we refer to as the passive learner. The learner simply satisfies the task through acts of inclusion, mimicry, or memorization. For instance, the student might simply follow directions to complete a task or might only imitate what the teacher does or parrot what the teacher says. The need for critical, reflective thinking, self-challenging thought, different perspectives, and self-reliance is nonexistent as the student proceeds through the scaffolded progression of learning. Passive learners might ignore feedback, which can lead to apathy or disconnectedness from learning.

Short-Term Application and Shallow Recall

Passive engagement with learning leads to short-term application of learning, which only demands a shallow recall of material. Research states that if we only cycle knowledge and skills through short-term application, we lessen the chance that these knowledge and skills stay in long-term memory. It is only when they embed themselves in long-term memory that a learner can begin to consolidate and construct learning that lasts (Brown, Roediger, & McDaniel, 2014). Think of a multiple-choice exam. These types of exams only ask that a student recognize the content or material when given contextual cues and choices. This is not the same as synthesizing the content or material into a new skill or new learning.

Time Bound

This linear, scaffolded instruction is typically built on the idea of short-term knowledge cycling and skill application in small, time-bound periods that supposedly culminate in an intended state of learning. The issue is that not all students learn at the same pace, and proficiency develops at different times. Deliberately chunking time in which students must learn all these small components devastates the very nature of growth and proficiency development.

Teacher Centered

Learning must be student focused, not teacher focused. This means that teachers must go beyond presenting students with information and material. Teacher-centered teaching is commonly described as "being the sage on the stage." In a teacher-centered approach, the teacher holds the information and content and then makes decisions on how and when to release that information to the students. We all know, however, that just because we taught it doesn't mean students have learned it.

Based on Gradual Release of Responsibility Model

Our most significant and serious concern with this traditional model of instruction involves the idea of gradual release. We believe that the gradual release model of lesson design and delivery does far more harm than good in promoting student learning and achievement. We must move away from the *I do*, *we do*, *you do* model of instruction and lesson design and rethink our traditional approach. Learning is not about imitation and is more than just practice. If we are truly working with skills that promote critical thinking and judgment, we need to consider classrooms that go beyond students restating or parroting what the teacher might say or do.

We are advocating for a fundamental shift in how teachers design instruction and lesson planning. Throughout this book, we build a case for a different lesson-planning model, one based on proficiency-based instruction. This model of lesson design and delivery is more effective in developing efficacy and proficiency because students are the primary generators of learning. In the traditional gradual release model, it is typically the teacher who initiates and generates student learning. In this model, students do not learn how to self-initiate, self-monitor, or self-sustain their own learning. They don't necessarily experience failure or setback, so they don't develop learning resilience, self-appraisal skills, and reflective stamina. All of these traits are essential to developing rooted proficiency, not merely the illusion of it.

Reinventing the Lesson Plan and Instructional Delivery

Since the work of Hunter (1982), a lot has changed in education, but the template or framework for building lesson plans and delivering instruction has not.

Schools have moved from textbooks to iPads, pencils to styluses, and overhead projectors to LCDs. We now have the internet, the capacity to create flipped classrooms, and online learning. We have resources and technologies that continue to be refined in order to provide engaging, vivid, and reflective learning experiences for students. More important, we have far more research about teaching and learning than we've ever had. We know more about *how* students learn. New research about brain development provides educators with greater insights than ever before. Education research has generated clarity around best practices and strategies, and we've broken down barriers to support the idea that all students can gain access to the best curriculum our schools can offer.

For these reasons and others, a critical look at how we instruct students is an important step toward rethinking and redesigning approaches to teaching and learning. A new and better model for instruction and lesson planning can help teachers integrate stronger, more informed, and current research practices that increase student engagement and achievement.

With a focus on the ability to develop skills and flexible proficiency with content, the practice of proficiency development is the norm of education. With all that being said, we need a new instructional framework to support this new idea of education. We call this *proficiency-based instruction*, which deliberately includes reflective interaction with students to develop competency.

Likewise, proficiency-based instruction is committed to fostering interdependence among collaborative teams—team structures that recognize the value of continuous improvement, strengthening each other's instructional delivery, and focusing on student results.

In This Book

The basic structure of this book follows the same basic format as our two previous proficiency-based books: *Proficiency-Based Assessment: Process, Not Product* (Gobble et al., 2016) and *Pathways to Proficiency: Implementing Evidence-Based Grading* (Gobble et al., 2017).

Chapter 1 outlines the foundation for implementing proficiency-based instruction: psychologist Mihaly Csikszentmihalyi's (1990) five stages of the creative process. Each stage focuses on a stage of development as teams work through their understanding of shifting to a proficiency-based instructional model for teaching and learning. The five stages include: (1) preparation, (2) incubation, (3) insight, (4) evaluation, and (5) elaboration.

Chapter 2 focuses on the preparation stage. In this chapter, we introduce a fictitious team of teachers as they collaborate to implement proficiency-based instruction in their classrooms. This team represents a number of teams we've worked with and combines the questions, concerns, and ideas that have emerged from many different teachers we've observed and collaborated with to make revisions to instructional practices.

The preparation stage is a deliberate period during the change process. During this stage, the team establishes clarity around the value and purpose of making a shift to proficiency-based instruction. This stage is educational. It helps the team compare and contrast traditional lesson planning with a proficiency-based approach to instruction, so it can logically interconnect lesson planning with other areas of teaching and learning focused on proficiency.

The preparation stage builds a working foundation for the incubation stage, which is the focus of chapter 3. The incubation stage is a time for open conversations about making the change to proficiency-based instruction and different ways teams can implement the change that is authentic and valuable to students.

The incubation stage leads to the insight stage, the focus of chapter 4. This stage is when aha moments occur and teams begin to see greater value in making a shift to proficiency-based instruction. These insights lead to genuine change, making an impact on student growth.

Chapter 5 continues with the team's journey, as they evaluate instructional shifts and revisions. In the evaluation stage, the team identifies and explores the effectiveness of their efforts and reflect on how instructional revisions are helping every student. These evaluative discussions forward the thinking of the team, encouraging them to elaborate on their ideas, the final stage of the process.

Chapter 6 covers the elaboration stage, which fosters collaboration in more specific and nuanced ways. During this stage, teams build off their efforts, continuously revising and improving their instruction.

Chapter 7 offers examples of proficiency-based lesson plans, including various templates, charts, and figures to help guide readers through the lesson-planning process.

Finally, chapter 8 explores real-world examples of discipline-specific, proficiency-based instruction in action.

Our intention with this book is to show how one teaching team works together for the benefit of all students and offers an example of what we can do to motivate better, more thoughtful changes in our work. As you will see, this team has moved beyond a one-size-fits-all model and, instead, they have designed and delivered more effective teaching and learning experiences that promote the growth of all students.

chapter 1

Implementing Proficiency-Based Instruction: Five Stages of the Creative Process

Collectively, we've observed thousands of classes and engaged in thousands of reflective conversations about teaching and learning. Within these observations and conversations, the best teaching practices recognize that students enter into every lesson from many different points in their learning and in irregular ways. In this book, we emphasize that instructional practices must maintain flexibility in order to reach all students, and instructional changes must happen immediately in order to ensure high levels of learning for all students. Instruction, like assessment and grading or reporting practices, must focus on developing the learner's proficiency.

Moving away from the Madeline Hunter (1982) tradition of structured lesson design, we examine instruction and lesson planning instead through the lens of proficiency, where all students can find themselves in a learning environment that nurtures individual, continuous improvement. By shifting our focus to each student's ability and developing proficiency, as opposed to a one-size-fits-all lesson plan, we address how we must reinvent instructional practices to be proficiency based.

Breaking away from the traditional approaches to teaching and learning requires thought, collaboration, and input. As in our other two books, we recognize that sustainable changes that reinvent instructional practices must come from a steady commitment to how we *prepare* for changing how we build lessons, *incubate* or brainstorm needed changes in lessons toward a proficiency-based model, create greater *insights* into every student's learning, *evaluate* or reflect on our lessons, and work with teams to *elaborate* on developing ideas.

Central to our work is a deep commitment to collective inquiry and collaboration. Teachers working in collaboration can lead to inventive and sustainable change. To create these smarter, more developed conversations, we subscribe to *go slow to go far* mindset. Sustainable change happens when teachers take their time to understand it and make sense of how it impacts instructional practice and student learning.

To effectively pace change and lead smarter, more effective conversations around teaching and learning, we rely on longstanding research grounded in the creative process. As previously discussed, Csikszentmihalyi (1990) presents the creative process in five interconnected and overlapping stages: (1) preparation, (2) incubation, (3) insight, (4) evaluation, and (5) elaboration. By building instructional changes around these five stages, we better prepare teachers to understand the principles of proficiency-based instruction and why it has a greater impact on students than traditional methods. We allow teachers to incubate ideas that connect the principles of proficiency-based instruction to their own lesson planning, gain insights, evaluate ideas, and elaborate on what is working or alter what does not. We are starting to see how teachers adapt their approach to instruction with proficiency as their core focus.

By intentionally addressing these five stages in the change process, teachers and teams receive better professional development that leads to a different approach to instruction, an approach that:

▸ Supports reasons to revise the approach to lesson design

▸ Recognizes the value of multiple viewpoints and input during the change process

▸ Provides specific environments that open up thinking and teachers' creative aha moments

▸ Encourages reflective professional development that addresses evaluation and discernment

▸ Develops a culture of continuous improvement and thoughtful revision

For purposes of simplicity, this book treats these five stages as if we are progressing through a team's journey to implement proficiency-based instruction. As in our other books, the stages first appear as separate events; however, as you will see, eventually all stages begin to overlap one another, occurring together, not separately. We map the progression of changes as they initially build off one another.

As you read, consider why each stage is important to developing long-lasting, sustained education commitments that build stronger instructional practices focused on each student's development and growth. More specifically, we hope to provide you with a pathway to implement proficiency-based instruction—a change that helps us incorporate the best and most recent research in teaching and learning.

Preparation

During the preparation stage, collaborative teams immerse themselves in new learning. They take the time to understand the ideas behind proficiency-based instruction and compare and contrast traditional models of lesson design against a model that focuses on individual student growth. During this stage, it is important to identify complex issues that are problematic or arouse curiosity and provide a foundational reason to problem solve and make the change.

In the case of teaching and learning, shifting to proficiency-based instruction means letting go of past practices, embracing change, and inventing a new approach to the classroom learning experience.

During the preparation stage, teams should consider the following.

▸ To establish a commitment to proficiency-based instruction, collaborative teams should compare and contrast longstanding approaches to lesson design with a proficiency-based approach. The collaborative team must be willing to question and challenge its current instructional practices and consider how to implement strategies that focus on proficiency.

▸ For purposes of equity, collaborative teams must be able to develop consensus around *how* students demonstrate proficiency during classroom instruction, what to do when students *are not* developing proficiency, and what to do when students *do* demonstrate proficiency.

▸ Teams should be able to reflect on their own practices, refer to evidence of student proficiency, and engage in discussions that support continuous improvement.

Incubation

The incubation stage refers to the period during which ideas churn and develop. After someone has started working on a solution to a problem or has had an idea leading to a novel approach, he or she enters the incubation stage. The incubation stage can last hours, days, months, or years, as it is often open ended and packed with a variety of ideas, thoughts, and deliberations.

During this stage, ideas percolate and thoughts come together in unexpected combinations that form domain-changing breakthroughs. This is important to recognize when shifting to proficiency-based instruction because collaborative teams often need this time to develop a stronger, more authentic commitment to a change. Individual teachers and teams need to make sense of the change, wrestle with ideas, and understand the value of the change in relation to past practices.

During the incubation stage, teams should consider the following.

▸ Authentic instructional design is key; the idea that instruction and assessment are one and the same creates authenticity. In this way, assessment helps teachers manage instructional changes more quickly so they can promptly address gaps in learning. A shift toward proficiency-based instruction requires patient incubation—it is a significant shift in practice, and educators need time to unpack the advantages of making the change and envision the possibilities it can create for students.

▸ Teams compare and contrast the new ideas that proficiency-based instruction promotes to longstanding, traditional instructional practices. In this stage, teams engage in a useful debate about making a change to proficiency-based instruction. They begin to consider how and why this shift can support positive changes in student learning.

▸ Team members need to help one another address their questions and concerns quickly. They need support and direction if they are incubating ideas that will form obstacles to this new instructional approach instead of advantages. When teams ask questions that challenge old practices, those questions are legitimate; however, the team might need clear responses from leaders who are able to better justify the value of making the shift. In other words, teams need a lot of leadership support as they incubate change.

▸ When teachers and leaders continually ask themselves, "Is this the best way we can do things?," it can signal to the staff, students, parents, and other stakeholders that the institution is in a place of growth and promise. When teams demonstrate their own willingness to grow and learn, others may follow. When teachers support a growth mindset in their own lives, that tendency can trickle into the classroom.

Teachers and leaders can maintain a focus on growth in their instructional practices by embracing the idea of reperformance, in which teachers give students the opportunity for retakes. In a proficiency-based model, learning is difficult to pace. Not every student learns at the same rate. By providing longer developmental windows, we can get better at supporting student learning over different windows of development and not shut down learning with arbitrary deadlines.

Insight

The insight stage is an exciting stage in the change process. It is the aha moment when the puzzle of proficiency-based instruction starts to come together. This stage is also called the "Eureka!" experience. It's the moment in time when a problem an individual has been trying to solve—for days, months, or years—makes sense in his or her mind and he or she forms a clear resolution. This often happens during team collaboration, when a teammate sees through a difficult challenge in teaching and learning and identifies an innovative solution. At these points, resolution often emerges after a complex and lengthy process, but that process creates meaningful change.

We encourage working with teams to help teachers develop their own insights into the value of proficiency-based instruction. When teachers fuel one another's thinking, they internalize and implement changes.

During the insight stage, teams should consider the following.

▶ Not all instructional choices make a positive impact on learning. Some instructional choices may even be counterproductive to learning.

▶ Proficiency-focused instructional practices create a lesson structure that provides immediate feedback on student learning and generates real-time instructional shifts to support student growth.

▶ Throughout a unit of study, high-functioning teams develop insights into better instructional practices when they spend time collaborating during the development of student learning.

▶ Collaborating to analyze and create instructional insights helps teams reach all students.

Evaluation

The purpose of the evaluation stage is to decide if an insight is valuable and worth pursuing. During the final stages of the creative process, individuals must decide if their insights will improve student learning. In other words, they must analyze the insights to determine if they are making an impact on results. If the insight continues to excite and motivate the individual to go forward, then the hard work of turning it into a reality begins.

For example, teachers might evaluate how they are opening a lesson to collect evidence of student proficiency. They might ask each other questions about how they can quickly gather assessment data and effectively and efficiently promote learning growth throughout the remainder of the lesson. Proficiency-based instruction depends heavily on data-driven, evaluation-based discussions. This helps teams pin down the effectiveness of their instructional efforts.

During the evaluation stage, teams should consider the following.

▶ Teachers who use proficiency-based instruction attend closely to evaluation, continually examining and responding to the learning needs of every student to ensure his or her development.

▶ Teams must commit to collaborating with one another around how they use instructional strategies that facilitate learning more effectively and efficiently.

▶ They should be mindful that they are examining how well instruction improves learning. Team conversations should be about instructional changes and action steps that lead to classroom learning.

▶ Openly evaluating and assessing proficiency-based instruction means dedicating themselves to continually examining the evidence of student learning and determining the value of instructional practices.

Elaboration

During the elaboration stage, teams revise ideas or add nuance. It's this stage of the change process that focuses on continuous growth and improvement. During this stage, teams should consider the following.

▶ Like each stage in the change process, the elaboration stage is about continuous improvement. Elaboration can be about fine-tuning or adding nuance to instructional changes, or it can involve effecting a bigger change, one that overhauls an approach to instruction.

▶ Teams will see the value of proficiency-based instructional practices and build on it or revise their ideas. At this point in the journey, team members are also ready to serve as teacher leaders, sharing their struggles and successes with other teacher teams that might also be working to change.

▶ At this point, the team works for continuous improvement and success for every student. Team members might ask the question, "Is this change working for every student or just a subgroup of students? How so? If not, how might the change be more beneficial for more learners?"

These five stages model the way we want to approach professional growth and positive changes in our schools as we work to build productive discussions around proficiency-based instruction. Each stage seeks the expertise, collaboration, and inquiry of educators. Making changes with the input of other experts is demanding, but the rewards for teaching and learning are exciting and extraordinarily valuable for students. By working through each stage, changes begin to make sense, evolve, and take root because educators spend time collaborating and consulting with one another each step of the way.

As the education profession seeks to address its many different and complex challenges, the creative process reminds us to be prepared for change, incubate change and not rush to decisions, generate insights into change, thoughtfully evaluate the changes we make, and continuously improve and evolve.

As this book unfolds, we break down how we use these five stages of the creative process to integrate proficiency-based instruction into the work of one team's journey. Each chapter dedicates itself to explaining a stage more fully, demonstrates change through the eyes of teachers, and identifies key strategies to support a change to proficiency-based instruction so you can take this process and replicate it in your own classroom, school, and district. As you'll see, each stage fosters powerful discussions around teaching and student learning.

Key Takeaways From Chapter 1

Review these key points with your team to reinforce the concepts from this chapter.

1. Teaching teams should understand why a shift to proficiency-based instruction is important to teaching and learning. Preparing for this shift helps teachers better connect with how proficiency-based instruction is interlocked with proficiency-based standards and assessment practices.

2. Provide time for teachers to incubate and brainstorm ideas that will help support the shift to proficiency-based instruction. This

can help teachers integrate their expertise as they make decisions about change.

3. Teams will have insights that can help them see how a shift to proficiency-based instruction is meant to support the development of all learners.

4. Be sure to evaluate the shift as teachers are implementing instructional changes. Reflective evaluation and evidence of student work can help teachers understand how instructional shifts are supporting student growth.

5. The elaboration stage helps support the ongoing mindset that instruction is a process of continuous improvement.

Stop, Think, Reflect

With your team, reflect on the following three questions to continue with the collaborative process for change.

1. What is the compelling *why* to shift to proficiency-based instruction?

2. What are the leadership challenges in supporting positive instructional changes?

3. How does your school encourage and celebrate a focus on positive, collaborative changes?

chapter 2

Preparation

This chapter focuses on how to introduce a teacher team to a proficiency-based instructional model. The preparation stage recognizes that change requires building a foundation for change. Teachers must be prepared to implement this change effectively. Before making the shift to a proficiency-based instructional model, teams need to understand why the change is important to teaching and learning, how the change can help support students, and what steps they need to take to succeed.

Following are three key points to remember during the preparation stage.

1. Teams should spend time learning about proficiency-based instruction and how it is connected to other education shifts, such as proficiency-based assessment and stronger, more immediate feedback practices. Seeing these interconnections can help to build a more unified understanding of the value of making the change and build off the previous knowledge teachers have about the concept of proficiency.

2. The preparation stage is meant to make sure teams are invested in the purpose of making the change. During this stage, teachers should focus on why this shift can help students learn and grow every day.

3. The preparation stage takes time. When teams are working to create change, they should take time to build a strong foundation. This leads teams to greater levels of insight, stronger ideas about teaching and learning, and more thoughtful approaches to helping every student succeed.

The preparation stage often requires ongoing support and clarity. As teachers are considering a new approach to lesson design, they will have some important questions and concerns. It is important to allow for these questions to develop a deeper understanding that supports the reasons why a shift to proficiency-based instruction is beneficial to the growth of all students and the value of each component of lesson design.

In making a shift to proficiency-based instruction, preparing to change often means stepping back to examine past practices. Looking at traditional lesson-planning models and comparing them to a model that reformats how we structure a lesson is an important first step (see table I.1, page 2). Doing so helps teams see more clearly how traditional lesson-planning models are not structured with the individual learner in mind. Teams can gain a greater understanding about how and why a proficiency-based instructional model is better for all students. This step causes teachers to examine how to improve on teaching and learning and why this change is so important, helping them recognize that sometimes improvements mean completely restructuring or overhauling what they've done for decades.

Educational choices generally, and instructional practices specifically, should embrace both equity and excellence. While we make decisions and revise how we approach teaching and learning, educators should keep those goals in mind. If we want to institutionalize a change, the change should lead to both equity and excellence for all students. A shift to proficiency-based instruction requires that teachers embrace such a collective commitment. Any change needs a compelling *why* behind it. Taking the time to examine the value behind a change to proficiency-based instruction helps to inspire an imperative toward positive change. The preparation stage helps teachers enter into that conversation thoughtfully and purposefully.

The preparation stage encourages teachers to see the change as something that supports a future of greater success for all students. It asks the key question, "What if?" By building *what if* discussions, we hope to create collaboration that feeds continuous improvement. For example:

▸ What if we approach our lessons with a better understanding of each student's proficiency level?

▸ What if we structure our lessons to promote collaboration as students develop their skills?

A thoughtful, committed conversation about proficiency-based instructional changes leads teachers to consider greater possibilities.

In the next part of this chapter, you will read the story of how one team grapples with the change to proficiency-based instruction. As you read about this team's journey, consider the ways team members prepare for change—learning first, comparing, contrasting, investigating, asking questions, and fleshing out each other's understanding. In doing so, the team collaborates to learn more about how its instructional approach leads students to develop their individual potential, proficiency, and mastery of learning.

As you read, listen to the educators in the story. We wrote them with some of our best teachers in mind—some early adopters, some willing to change, some questioning change, and some waiting for others to adopt changes first. When reading, presume positive intent. Each teacher is a change agent. What does each change agent need? How do teachers and teacher leaders support teams in their efforts early in the change process? How is confidence toward change developing?

As you read the team's story, consider the following three challenges of preparing to understand and implement proficiency-based instruction.

1. Are all team members fully committed to the purpose of proficiency-based instruction, and do they realize how the change connects to the collective commitment to excellence and equity?

2. Is the team paying close attention to how a change to proficiency-based instruction compares and contrasts to past lesson-planning structures?

3. Is the team identifying ways in which a shift to proficiency-based instruction can better incorporate current research that communicates better practices in teaching and learning?

Our Team's Story

In the past, Marcos, Lauren, Nico, Tony, and Sofie started each school year with the same dedicated focus. As a team, they wanted to work together to make sure their lessons were engaging for students. They met to exchange and share ideas about teaching and learning and generate lesson plans together. One of their priorities was to create lessons with introductory activities that would hook students into learning and then build high-interest activities. Many of their lessons followed a commitment to gradual release of responsibility, in which they would model learning and then allow students to work independently. As a team, they enjoyed meeting with one another. They were goal-driven and dedicated to building lessons collaboratively.

This year, the team members wanted to spend time addressing concerns tied to their instructional delivery. Despite their focus on building positive relationships with students and engaging lesson activities, many of their students were still struggling to meet the team's stated expectations. They were having success with a number of students in their classes, but in the past few years, they had not reached their goal to ensure all students were meeting proficiency. The team knew it needed to confront some serious questions about whether all students were actually learning, and the team leader, Marcos, had spent his summer pulling together materials to help open up this discussion. The team had created its proficiency scales, but it hadn't worked on how its instructional practices were working in the classroom to develop each student's competencies.

Marcos opened the first meeting of the year by reviewing the team norms of giving input openly and honestly and remaining open to new ideas that might challenge current practices. After vetting the norms, Marcos moved to the next item on the agenda, reviewing the student data results from the previous few years. He referred to this activity as the *student data autopsy*, in which team members look at last year's students, review how they performed, and discuss why they think some students didn't achieve to the level they had hoped. There was some cause for celebration, but there also was some cause for concern. About 35 percent of students had moved on to the next grade without meeting the team's expectations. They had not met their goal, and the data showed little movement in the right direction.

Lauren, Nico, Tony, and Sofie reviewed the data and agreed that they needed to focus on changes in their instructional approach. Nico spoke up first: "We've been working really hard every year. I'm interested in looking more closely at what we are doing in the classroom to promote change. If the students are engaged in the lesson, I'm not sure why they aren't learning."

"I know what you mean, Nico," Lauren agreed. "When we look at these data, I'm not impressed with our outcomes. We are all working hard, but I think we need to work differently with our students."

Marcos noted, "I know we might be disappointed, but I think we need to build off our strengths and recommit to how we can improve the work we do in the classroom. Last year, we discussed adapting our work to address how our instruction could focus on developing proficiency on a day-to-day basis, and we spent time at the end of the year reading about creating classroom lessons that focused more on developing student proficiency during a class period. I hope you had time this summer to think through some ideas around proficiency-based instruction, and I'm hopeful we can start to collaborate around this idea, make sense of it, and adapt this approach to our teaching."

Sofie said, "I understand what you are saying, Marcos, and I did think about what we read and discussed at the end of last year. In looking at these data, I'm frustrated that we are looking at our concerns *now* for the students of last year. I want to spend more time this year looking at our concerns about students while we can still help them. I think proficiency-based instruction asks us to do that. One thing we discussed last year was spending more time focusing in on instructional changes every week, so we are reviewing what we need to improve more immediately in the classroom."

Tony nodded in agreement. "I know what you mean, Sofie. Our team spends a lot of time discussing our curriculum, learning targets, and assessments. I think we need to discuss why our instruction isn't supporting our students' learning. I teach everything we discuss; I try to use our differentiated instructional techniques; and I try to be engaging. I know all of you do, too. However, I'm concerned that our team is so focused on teaching that we are not focused on what students are actually learning—or not learning. I think some of our differentiated instructional techniques work, but our data show that our students aren't learning to the degree we had hoped."

Lauren pointed out an observation in the data: "That's right, Tony. From the data, I'm noticing that some students are just staying stagnant, even the ones who are doing well. Does anyone else notice that too? Look. A number of students started as proficient and ended as proficient. I guess we can call that *good*, but I don't think we should feel great about those data either, since they don't show growth."

"I noticed that too," Nico said. "It seems like we aren't helping the students who are struggling enough, that's obvious. But we also aren't helping the students who aren't struggling. From my understanding, proficiency-based instruction works to make sure *all* students progress in their learning. I think that contrasts with traditional approaches to lesson planning that teach to specific objectives."

Marcos said, "I'm glad you're all noticing those concerns. I noticed them, too. I think in the past, we've been focused on some important elements of our work as a team; however, I think we forgot to confront a really important question along the way. Are *all* students learning? This year, I think we need to dedicate ourselves to paying closer attention to our instruction as well as what Lauren and Nico noticed. We need to make sure we are developing the potential of every student every day, in every lesson. I think a shift to proficiency-based instruction can help guide our collaboration so we are building lessons with learning as the focus. Personally, when I compare the proficiency-based instructional model with our traditional lesson planning, I think a shift in how we instruct should logically align to all the other work we've been doing around developing proficiency-based assessments and the way we've discussed scaled learning targets."

Marcos continued, "One of the first things we need to discuss is that students' competencies are all very different whenever they step into the classroom."

Sofie said, "I sure know that. The students I had last year were so different from one another. In my classroom, I had days when some students knew everything I was teaching and some students seemed to be hearing it for the first time. The range of learning was huge."

"You weren't alone," Nico said. "Some of my students had no background knowledge. Luckily, I had a few students I could count on to help work with other students. I think the shift to a proficiency-based instructional model will help me to move all students forward in our gradations for learning. The shift will help me to focus more on how every student can grow in his or her learning throughout the lesson and throughout the school year."

"That's right," Marcos replied. "I think it's normal for there to be a range of student learning in the classroom. There is a difference in students' competencies. Moreover, those competencies fluctuate. Sometimes a student is doing well, and sometimes he or she is struggling. In teaching, we tend to forget that. We think all students come into the class the same, and it is our job to make sure they all leave at the same endpoint. That idea just isn't true."

Marcos proceeded to draw the following two figures on the chalkboard (see figures 2.1 and 2.2).

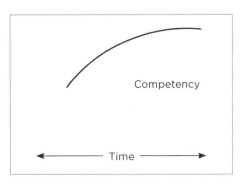

Source: Jain & Reibel, 2018.

Figure 2.1: Common view of competency development.

Source: Jain & Reibel, 2018.

Figure 2.2: How competency develops.

Marcos explained, "The first graph shows how we traditionally look at developing students' competencies. We presume that students come to class needing to learn our stated learning targets. We assume they come in not knowing, and it is our job to grow their learning. The second graph is a better way to look at student competency. The second graph shows the reality of how learning and competency happen. In this graph, students enter into a lesson with many different ability levels."

"That's a great observation," Sofie said. "In getting our teaching degrees, I think we all learned to develop a lesson plan with the first graph in mind, not the second graph. Ever since I was a student teacher, I've been building lesson plans for the first graph, and our team has been building our lessons that way, too. To be blunt, we build lessons assuming the students know nothing."

Marcos nodded his head in agreement. "Right, and instead, what we should be doing is building lessons that meet students where they are when they come to class and progress their learning during the class period. The traditional lessons we've been developing are helping some of our students but not all of them."

Nico looked surprised. "Wait a second. Does this mean the lessons we've been building for years don't work?"

Lauren said, "Well, it doesn't mean they don't work. But it does mean that we should question whether our lessons work for all students, and we should probably examine whether our lessons are promoting growth or stagnation."

"This discussion makes logical sense. It does," Tony added. "I've had many teaching experiences where I know some students are bored and under-challenged. I build my lesson plans around the learning targets, not the gradations for learning. I create lessons to teach to the middle. I don't build lessons to support the developing proficiencies of all students. I teach all students the same thing at the same time and then grade them."

Marcos replied, "That's an important point in our discussion, isn't it? Imagine if you were learning piano and you switched teachers. What if your second piano teacher just made you relearn what you already knew? You'd remain stagnant in your learning. Or, what if your second piano teacher tried to teach you something too advanced and then failed you for not being able to demonstrate advanced skills? Our daily lesson planning is structured similarly to the mistakes of that second piano teacher. If we don't create lessons that support the learning differences in the room, we are either promoting stagnation or failure."

Lauren said, "I agree. We've been teaching like there is a clear, neat, sequential pathway for all students to follow, as if they are all the same. Isn't that what we were all taught in college? And isn't that the way curriculum guides and textbooks are structured, as if we should build learning step by step and page by page?"

"Lauren makes a good point," agreed Sofie. "Student learning isn't as neat and orderly as traditional ideas of education make it out to be. Learning isn't sequential. Often it is messy and nonlinear. I think a shift to proficiency-based instruction asks us to think differently."

Marcos sensed the group was beginning to recognize a number of concerns with its instructional practices. He said, "I think we are already ahead of ourselves in our agenda."

Tony replied, "If you're wondering if we are interested in making a shift to how our students are developing, then I think we are interested in focusing our lessons on proficiency-based instruction. One thing I think we could do is consider whether we give students enough time to develop the competencies we are asking from them. In looking at the data, we aren't remembering that students learn at different paces."

Marcos nodded and said, "That's one of the more important points in proficiency-based instruction. In this approach, the starting point and ending point are different for each student. We might teach, but some students might not be learning."

Sofie added, "So, I think we might need to consider how we can attend to each student's developing proficiency during the class period, rather than just engaging students in the same activity."

Marcos said, "If we take these graphs more seriously, we will want to revise our lessons."

"A *lot*...," Nico agreed, "but I don't think we need to scrap what we've been doing, we just need to think differently about how we approach the instructional components of our work."

Tony said, "Yes, this isn't a complete overhaul, but it is a commitment. To me, it means starting our classes differently by first paying attention to how our students enter the room."

Nico replied, "Yes and then determining how a student is growing or not growing during the class period. By collecting evidence immediately, we are able to constantly assess students and progress their development."

Marcos said, "Right. So, during our next meeting, let's really start to brainstorm. Let's spend some time thinking about what we are learning and observing as we start preparing to implement this change. When we come together next time, we can explore our different perspectives and ideas."

Two Commitments of Proficiency-Based Instruction

A shift to proficiency-based instruction means making two important commitments to teaching and learning.

1. Recognize the true nature of teaching and learning, understanding that it is not a one-size-fits-all process. This commitment is important as it enables us to break away from traditional lesson planning.

2. Embrace the concept of *student efficacy*, recognizing that students need to be involved in their own reflective growth process during learning opportunities.

If teams make these two foundational commitments, a much richer, inventive discussion of teaching and learning can develop, focusing on individualized student growth.

Commitment 1: Recognize the True Nature of Teaching and Learning

Merriam-Webster defines *learning* as "knowledge or skill acquired by instruction or study" (Learning, n.d.). This limited definition of learning leads to many of the issues we see in education today: passive students, poor grading systems, hyper-focus on pacing, and unclear expectations around achievement. It has led us from what we consider the real definition of learning to be: the development of proficiency.

A teacher's responsibility is to teach the curriculum that matches what we want students to know, understand, and be able to do during a school year. However, as noted earlier, just because we taught it doesn't mean students learned it. When we consider the relationship between teaching and learning, we must pay close attention to both sides of the relationship. We want to make sure that through effective teaching, students learn. Proficiency-based instruction focuses on that commitment.

Proficiency-Based Learning Defined

One of the primary goals of education has been for students to develop competencies and proficiencies related to specific curricular goals or personal goals. So why has the traditional definition of learning permeated our education system for so long? Why hasn't proficiency rather than content been at the center of our pedagogy? When we define learning from a proficiency development perspective, we get a very different definition of learning. We define *proficiency-based learning* with the following five components.

1. **It co-constructs learning around evidence:** Both students and teachers construct and build learning around the evidence students produce through reflective dialogue. Both parties mutually develop a student's competency, which in turn helps the student become a more self-regulated and self-reliant learner. The idea of

co-constructing learning solidifies the chances for effective growth and learning.

2. **It is based in kinship rather than autocracy:** Teaching out of kinship rather than autocracy is an important mindset for helping students discover their true potential. When a teacher acts alongside a student as he or she develops competency, the student sees the teacher as a "formative friend," and a safe and trusting learning relationship can blossom. This is similar to what Michelle E. Cardwell (2011) notes about teachers when they support autonomy during the learning process.

   When the teacher can successfully achieve the role of mentor instead of teacher, the resulting feedback becomes more mutually constructed and validating. The burden of reflection and self-appraisal is on the student. Developing self-reliance can critically influence a student's learning. Learning has the chance then to become much more self-guided and personal for the student.

3. **It creates personalized learning:** To develop proficiency and learning in the most effective way, teachers should aim to create the most intimate learning relationships possible. *Intimate* means that the teacher must use the student's state of mind and generated evidence as much as possible. When a teacher uses a student's work, thoughts, words, products, and so on to drive lessons, the student might feel that learning is happening organically through his or her relationship with the teacher, as opposed to using the prepared thoughts, content, and exemplars provided in many lesson guides. This learning intimacy builds trust, increases the likelihood of effective reflective conversations, and helps the student again to develop a trust in themselves, which ultimately leads to the development of self-efficacy.

4. **It embraces the natural oscillation of learning:** Learning is not a linear progression upward but rather an oscillating state of dissonance that eventually settles into a state of steady competence. Proficiency-based learning embraces this natural fluctuation, while the traditional view has attempted to avoid it. Teachers can effectuate the idea of embracing failure, grit, and perseverance only when they plan lessons that act in accordance with the idea that learning is messy. It eventually becomes un-messy as we allow for students' innate experiential exploration of learning.

5. **It promotes efficacy:** When teachers allow students to build their proficiencies and become aware of the realistic states of these proficiencies, their abilities to learn and grow can blossom. The realization that they can succeed when responsible for their own learning creates confidence. And this confidence in one's ability to grow oneself toward goals is efficacy (Hattie & Yates, 2014). Correlation between efficacy and achievement is well documented by experts such as John Hattie (2012) and Albert Bandura (1982) and is a valuable byproduct of proficiency development.

In summary, proficiency-based learning doesn't simply ask students to learn things but rather to become confident in the development of skills and content that allows them to achieve their goals. Alvin Toffler's (1970) observation rings true about the speed of changes in the modern workforce:

> By instructing students how to learn, unlearn, and relearn, a powerful new dimension can be added to education. . . . Tomorrow's illiterate will not be the man who can't read; he will be the man who has not learned how to learn. (p. 414)

It is the confidence in their ability to shift and grow their own learning that allows students to fully develop proficiency, and it is this development that is largely associated with one's realized accomplishments and life satisfaction.

What Proficiency-Based Learning Looks Like

We have just stated that we believe students learn by developing proficiencies and then nurturing confidence in those proficiencies. Thus the next logical question is, What is proficiency and how does one develop it?

Our exploration begins with the idea that for years, educators have assumed that the nature of instruction aligns perfectly with that of learning, but upon closer examination it really doesn't (Jain & Reibel, 2018). The current view of teaching and learning assumes that all students are in some state of deficiency and need to be brought to a state of proficiency. Let's take another look at the common view of competency development in figure 2.1 (page 24).

This image represents the entrenched belief that it is the *teacher's* skill in breaking down learning into parts, planning engaging activities, and providing feedback in a structured, guided manner that eliminates this lack of knowledge or learning. However, it is actually the *student's* skill in removing this lack of knowledge or learning, which teachers must develop and sustain.

Understanding learning in this way changes the nature of how we should approach designing and delivering instructional experiences for our students.

Proficiency-based learning recognizes that learning is volatile and oscillating at first and then eventually settles down into a functional state. These swings and oscillations are natural, and teachers must embrace them and understand that as time goes on and students move closer to a state of proficiency, the oscillations become less drastic and smaller in scale, and eventually nonexistent. The level at which a student can do this is the level and rate at which they learn. Let's look back at figure 2.2 (page 24), which shows a graph representing proficiency-based learning.

Ultimately, we want teaching to feel less like a ladder and more like a wave. In other words, we don't assume that students are in some state of nonproficiency and *climb* into a state of proficiency. Rather, in proficiency-based learning we understand that students are always in some state of proficiency, one that is constantly fluctuating as they interact and reflect with feedback, peers, teachers, and evidence. Through proper implementation of proficiency-based instruction, assessment, and grading, students will develop a stable state of any proficiency. Once in this state, students can refine their proficiency-based understanding of content and skills and will be more likely to flexibly learn, unlearn, and relearn in any situation.

Commitment 2: Embrace the Concept of *Student Efficacy*

Typically, we see students' confidence grow as they become more competent in a task or learning. As students become more adept at performing tasks or skills or seeing their knowledge benefit them in some way, they become more confident in themselves, as shown in figure 2.3.

When this confidence builds, the natural byproduct is personal efficacy. Two experts define personal efficacy in the following ways.

1. "Beliefs in one's capabilities to organize and execute the courses of action required to produce given attainments" (Bandura, 1997, p. 3)

2. "The confidence or strength of belief that we have in ourselves that we can make our learning happen" (Hattie, 2012, p. 41)

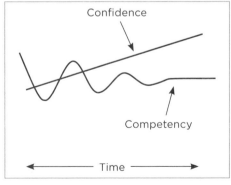

Source: Reibel, 2018a.

Figure 2.3: Competency and its relation to confidence.

According to Bandura (1997), personal efficacy has many documented benefits. It encompasses traits, such as work ethic, grit, and resilience; benefits also include:

▸ Healthy actions and choices

▸ Increased effort

▸ Perseverance

▸ Ability to handle adversity

▸ Healthy thought patterns

▸ Lower stress and depression

▸ Increased level of realized accomplishments

As we close this chapter, the questions remain: What learning do we really want? Do we want learning as the dictionary defines it, for students to simply come to know or possess isolated skills? Or do we want learning that helps students realize they can grow their own proficiencies? We believe the latter is the learning we should be striving for in our classrooms and schools.

Key Takeaways From Chapter 2

Review these key points with your team to reinforce the concepts from this chapter.

1. As teachers begin to prepare to make a shift to proficiency-based instruction, they must embrace the mindset that lesson planning cannot be a one-size-fits-all model. Proficiency-based instruction begins with the recognition that students are at different points in their learning; it is the teacher's responsibility to develop the skill level of each student.

2. An essential component in proficiency-based instruction is a focus on student self-reflection and efficacy, in which students learn to self-monitor their learning progression and growth. Nurturing this ability in students is central to the purpose of making the shift to proficiency-based instruction.

Stop, Think, Reflect

With your team, reflect on the following four questions to continue with the collaborative process for change.

1. How might your team compare and contrast proficiency-based instruction with traditional lesson-planning models? What is similar? What is different?

2. How does your team view a shift to proficiency-based instruction as purposeful and meaningful to student learning?

3. What might be an easy way to get started? How might your team try to implement proficiency-based instructional practices and learn by doing?

4. How is your team thinking about how the shift to proficiency-based instruction can work best for your students? How can this approach nurture a classroom environment with a focus on every student's learning?

chapter 3

Incubation

This chapter focuses on how a change to a proficiency-based instructional model requires questioning, thought, and critical analysis. In our experiences, teams need time to think about change, make sense of the change, and interconnect the change with their own expertise. Before making the shift to a proficiency-based instructional model, teams need to compare and contrast the differences between traditional lesson planning and the proficiency-based instructional model.

At this point in our team's journey to proficiency-based instruction, after developing a sturdy foundation during the preparation stage, our team now enters the incubation stage. During the incubation stage, teams should work through their own concerns while leaders support their developing understanding of the value of building lessons differently.

Following are three key points to remember during the incubation stage.

1. During this stage of teacher and team learning, authentic instructional design is key. We create that authenticity with the idea that instruction and assessment are one and the same. A shift toward proficiency-based instruction requires patient incubation—it is a significant shift in practice, and educators need time to unpack the advantages of making the change and to envision possibilities the change can create for students.

2. Teams build off comparing and contrasting longstanding, traditional instructional practices they investigated in the preparation stage and engage in useful debate. Reviewing past practices can lead to questioning and confusion, which might reveal a lack of clarity or the need to return to the preparation stage.

3. Team members need to help one another during this stage to have their questions and concerns addressed quickly. They need support and direction if they are incubating obstacles to this new instructional approach instead of incubating advantages. When teams ask questions that challenge old practices, those questions are legitimate; however, they need clear responses that make sense and are tied to the proficiency idea driving this change.

During the incubation stage, the team unpacks all the advantages and obstacles regarding proficiency-based instruction. This is also a time for making connections and clarifying concepts around the change. Some teams find it useful to brainstorm or brain dump during this stage, debating, wondering, and asking what-if questions. Some see it as a time for generating ideas around the change.

This stage contains all those activities, but incubation also strives to go a bit deeper. When incubating a change to proficiency-based instruction, individuals and teams should collaborate and focus on the many possibilities for *positive* change. They should explore how new choices can integrate logically into lesson design. At this point, educators need to keep an open mind and continue to ask themselves, "What's best for students? How will this shift toward proficiency-based instruction create an impact?"

During the incubation stage, ideas both good and bad percolate. As in our other two books, we encourage individuals and teams to take the time and latitude to bounce around ideas, consider, reconsider, question, mull over, and discuss. Teams should weigh these thoughts against past practices and fully explore how better, recent research informs the design of lessons that promote learning for all students. In doing so, individuals and teams make stronger choices about proficiency-based instructional practices. The individual or the team better understands the shift in practice because they've had the time to connect their own expertise to the change.

The incubation stage is a significant step for any individual or team because it encourages dissonance, by which we mean a break from longstanding beliefs, commitments, and structural templates that were ingrained and never deeply questioned. This stage takes some time. In asking teachers to rethink the way they lesson plan, a shift to proficiency-based instruction is asking them to reconceive a teaching career of practices that generations have followed without pausing and reconsidering. Often, individuals and teams struggle during this stage because it seems like too much change. They may need clarification, guidance in working through attainable action steps, and reassurance. Likewise, they may need to go back into the preparation stage and revisit research that helps them consider the way new education research supports a shift to a proficiency-based approach to teaching and learning. Teams might need to reread, collect data, or seek out other expertise for guidance.

Throughout the incubation stage, individuals and teams should begin to connect the dots. Team members should collaborate with one another to connect with the *why* behind the change to proficiency-based instruction and be able to identify possibilities for how the change can better support student learning. They should be able to think of ways to integrate a change.

As you read the story about our team's journey through the incubation stage, ask yourself, "How is the team interacting with the critical and challenging questions that may appear in this stage? What ideas about instructional practices are percolating during this stage? In what ways are we generating ideas to support the change to proficiency-based instruction?"

As you read the team's story, pay attention to the following three challenges around how our team is thinking during the incubation stage.

1. In what ways does the team begin to see how proficiency-based targets and gradations for learning interact with instructional lesson design?

2. How are teams building formative assessments into lesson design so that instructional choices support evidence of student learning?

3. How does content fit into a proficiency-based instructional model, and how are team members nurturing essential skills?

Our Team's Story

After the first meeting, the team reviewed the concepts of shifting to proficiency-based instruction, met informally to help one another with questions, and listed some of their concerns. The biggest concern team members had was breaking with past practices. After all, they were all very comfortable with the traditional style of lesson planning. Shifting in a new direction seemed daunting, and they felt a bit unsure. Marcos, the team leader, set up his agenda to address these concerns. He thought it would be a good idea for the team members to brainstorm their thoughts together; they would benefit from creating ideas that could help them approach the change to a more competency-based classroom.

At the meeting, Lauren started: "Marcos, I've been thinking a lot about this concept of the wave graph. I can see how it helps us visualize how learning happens, but I'm struggling to see how we can improve on what we are already doing. I have students who reflect on their learning, and I have students practice the competency, but I don't see how we can make this happen more than we already do now."

Marcos said, "Lauren, I understand what you're saying, and I think it is a really interesting observation. I think we've been making a number of good adjustments to our teaching over the last few years. We've been working to incorporate a number of thoughtful, research-based strategies, and we've been trying to keep up with best practices. I think the shift to a proficiency-based model embraces those important changes we've made. However, I think the proficiency-based instructional model requires us to consider how we are structuring those changes in our daily lessons.

"In the past, we've just been adding new instructional techniques and trying to cram them into the traditional lesson-planning template. Proficiency-based instruction requires that we reconsider the structure of our lesson plans so our best practices in teaching and learning work logically to produce greater results in student learning. I think our traditional lesson-planning model helped us teach lessons through a mode of modeling and presentation."

Nico finished Marcos's thought: "But the proficiency-based instructional model focuses on the students developing competency during the class period and through the course."

Sofie said, "I thought about it that way, too. This past week, I spent some time comparing and contrasting the traditional lesson-planning model I use in relation to a model that aligns to developing student competency. When I did that, I started to see the differences more clearly and how student reflection could work more successfully in a model focused on proficiency-based instruction. If we lay out the time line for a current lesson, we see the following progression." Sofie then drew the time line on the board (see figure 3.1).

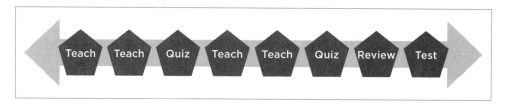

Figure 3.1: Traditional lesson time line.

Lauren said, "I see what you mean, Sofie. In that model, we teach and we teach and then we quiz on the small parts. Then, we teach and teach again, and then quiz again. At the end, we review all the small parts and make students take a big test to demonstrate if they learned everything in the unit."

"Yes," agreed Tony, "and that traditional model is aligned to that ladder-like graph, showing that we teach students the small pieces little by little until we finally ask them to pull the learning together at the end and show us that they know what we want them to know. On the other hand, if I understand this correctly, we should be building our lessons with the knowledge that learning fluctuates. We should consider assessments as formative and not grade them. Instead, we should be using the formative assessments to coach learning."

Marcos explained, "From what I've been reading, formative assessment is not just a series of small checks on something. Instead, on a writing assignment for example, formative assessment is more like the components of essay writing in which learning to write more effectively is a process that takes trial and error. Our job is to provide effective formative feedback along the way. In other words, the purpose of the lesson is more about developing competency."

Nico said, "But I thought the definition of formative assessment was to use assessments for feedback purposes."

Marcos replied, "Yes, that's true, but we want to consider how formative assessments help students self-reflect on their developing competency and how we need to make immediate instructional changes. We should use formative assessments to support more immediate change and help our team build more effective conversations about how student data inform instruction."

The team members agreed. Lauren said, "So, I think we need to think about how we outline our lessons to build off the formative development of student learning, especially for keeping competency at the forefront of our instructional practices." Lauren then drew a different time line on the board. "If we reconsider our unit design, I think it might look more like this" (see figure 3.2).

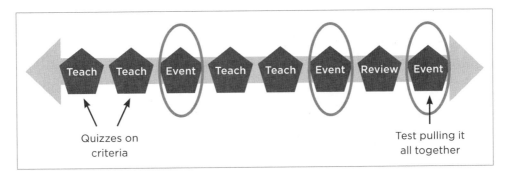

Figure 3.2: Proficiency-aligned lesson time line.

As Lauren was writing, Marcos added, "I think you are capturing some really good ways to approach proficiency-based instruction. From the way I understand it, the formative assessments have low stakes and help students demonstrate the components of learning lesson by lesson. Then, as they begin to build enough competency, they begin to make more skillful connections throughout the unit, demonstrating how the competencies work together to build a piece of writing more effectively. In the past, we didn't really view formative assessment and feedback in that way. We viewed it as a way to give students grades instead of allowing them to actually develop."

"If we try and connect this back to the wave graph (see figure 2.2, page 24), when we're *developing* our instruction, students are riding the wave and should not have any learning consequence, such as a final evaluation," Sofie pointed out.

Marcos agreed, "Yes, formative assessment should allow students to explore their learning and fluctuate as they work to become more proficient at a skill. During that time, we are providing feedback, and our instructional efforts help them develop their skills more fully and consistently. The graph recognizes that skills fluctuate. For instance, even the best tennis players have a bad serve from time to time. When students are working to demonstrate their skills, we need to remember that, especially when we are teaching something like writing a paper. Not every sentence is going to be strong, but what we want to see is the consistency of skillful writing, and we want to find evidence of those competencies."

"Really, any moment can be a viable assessment," said Tony, "but formative assessments occur as we are working to make sure all students are developing to meet our agreed-upon expectations. We need to move away from grading those formative assessments and allow them to be tools that help us coach students along the learning continuum of each. They will also inform us how we can better develop our instructional strategies."

Marcos said, "One challenge in this shift is to make sure we are providing students with formative assessments that we can integrate into a lesson in ways that support learning for all students."

Lauren added, "I've noticed that we often have expectations of students on assessments when we never actually taught them to develop the skills. For example, we might have students practice the steps for evaluating a source, but we rarely have them actually evaluate a source prior to the exam. If we incorporate more formative assessment practices, I think we will be able to develop every learner as we are working to monitor the evidence of every student's progress."

Tony said, "This is similar to when I coached basketball. We had practice drills, held scrimmages, and played games. The team always experienced the most development during the scrimmages. Learning seems to take place more deeply when students experience a simulation of the ultimate experience."

"Or, to think about it another way," Nico added, "we will build moments in which students are rehearsing small chunks of a play and have a few dress rehearsals before opening night."

Lauren asked, "What do you think our next steps in this process should be?"

Marcos replied, "Well, I think we should spend some time reflecting on how we can approach instruction differently than we've done in the past, and plan a unit and lessons focused on developing student proficiency. We should draft some examples of how we can test drive this model."

"I like that idea," Tony said. "Let's begin planning a lesson we can use early in the school year. I'd like to make sure my students begin the year recognizing that my job is to support and develop their potential, and their job is to demonstrate evidence of growth over time."

Marcos closed the meeting with an action step. "What I'm hearing is that we are going to work at making this shift. Let's find the time to work together and collaborate over some of our lesson revisions for the first unit. When we meet as a team again, we can review how we are re-approaching lesson design and share our developing insights. Let's take this slow. If we can figure this out in an effective way, I'm sure we will get more efficient at this work."

Nico said, "Right, Marcos. Let's go slow to go far."

Four Common Questions About Proficiency-Based Instruction

When implementing proficiency-based instruction, some unexpected questions might pop up. The most common include the following four questions.

1. What is the role of assessment?

2. What is the role of a standard or learning target?

3. Should my classroom be content focused or competency focused?

4. What is an anticipatory set, and what does it look like in proficiency-based instruction?

Question 1: What Is the Role of Assessment?

It is important for students to articulate when they are learning, how they are learning, and if they can understand how their development can lead to greater achievement and lifelong growth. As with proficiency-based assessment and evidenced-based grading, proficiency-based instruction aims to help students understand how to grow their own learning in more immediate ways.

There are three major uses for assessment within a proficiency-based instructional model: (1) deliver (developing supporting and prerequisite skills), (2) develop (developing student proficiency), and (3) determine (evaluating student proficiency).

Deliver (Developing Supporting and Prerequisite Skills)

Supporting assessments are assessments that teachers do not grade or rank. Teachers use this segment of instruction to develop supporting and prerequisite skills that students must rely on during the next segment of proficiency development.

This segment is entirely based on feedback and *nongraded* manipulation of content and skill components. We have never felt it important that a teacher score and classify the granular aspects of student work and give each and every component a grade. In the delivery segment of assessment, it is also important to note that this aspect of instruction is extremely low or no stakes. When teachers don't rank, students can embrace failed attempts without consequence. These assessment and instructional segments are formative, and teachers load them into a preparedness log section of the gradebook and *not* in the proficiency evaluation segment of the gradebook.

Develop (Developing Student Proficiency)

In the develop segment of proficiency-based instruction, teachers should focus primarily on creating and developing student proficiency. There are several key differences here from traditional instructional practice. First, teachers do grade and rank assessments during this segment. This allows students to fully contextualize their proficiency and determine if their emerging proficiency is appropriate for the moment.

Second, while instruction and assessment can look and feel any way the teacher wants them to, the assessments in the develop segment must mirror the summative moments in the grade level or course. For example, if the summative assessment asks students to write a narrative about a historical event, then during the develop segment of instruction and assessment, we should be explicitly helping students develop the skill of narrative writing. This alignment with a summative proficiency evaluation allows for a more accurate student self-assessment as well as detailed reflection about the desired state of proficiency (where the student's proficiency level is expected to be at the end of the learning cycle). These instructional segments and assessment events are formative and entered as inactive items in the gradebook.

Determine (Evaluating Student Proficiency)

In the determine segment of proficiency-based instruction, teachers create opportunities for students to produce evidence that they can directly review and judge against a desired state of proficiency (typically level 3 of a proficiency scale). In this segment of instruction and assessment, teachers often determine the current status, and perhaps the final status, of a student's proficiency.

When students are developing proficiency, they should be allowed to learn from their experiences without the fear of judgement. Assessments during this time are low or no stakes, which means teachers don't use them in their final judgment of student proficiency. They use them to monitor and encourage developing proficiency.

Teachers use this high-stakes segment of instruction as a summative evaluation to determine a student's proficiency against a state of desired proficiency. This creates conversations that result in a determination, or judgement of sorts, of a student's state of learning.

Teachers use evidence to determine a final grade or status for a learning target or a course. It is important to note that proficiency evaluations are not summative experiences. There can be multiple summative experiences that give the teacher and students an enhanced and clearer perspective in a learning conversation. They may occur several times in the course of one's learning experience; however, they are not the end to learning. They simply provide a guidepost. These assessment events and instructional segments are evaluative, and teachers load them into the gradebook as active items, or items used to determine the student's grade (keeping in mind, of course, that grades may change again when students finally demonstrate proficiency).

As teachers organize their lessons and units around proficiency, we suggest they first consider *all* moments in their class as viable evidence indicating developing proficiency. Assessment is not the only way, as shown in table 3.1 (page 42).

It is important to note that teachers can place *any* event in any of these columns. They can use homework for a deliver or a determine event; it just depends on what type of instructional segment they connect it to. See figure 3.3 (page 42) for an example.

Table 3.1: The Assessment Purpose of Proficiency-Based Learning

Deliver	Develop	Determine
Preparing For [Standard]	**Experience [Standard]**	**Evaluate [Standard]**
1. Assessments that are not marked, not graded 2. Used to develop prerequisite skills 3. Creates foundational knowledge 4. Used for feedback 5. Low or no stakes	1. Assessments that are marked, not graded 2. Used to experience and explore proficiency 3. Mimics the proficiency experience 4. Promotes self- and teacher awareness, reflection, appraisal skills 5. Low or no stakes	1. Assessments that are graded 2. Used to determine proficiency 3. Judges a mastery experience 4. Creates accurate self-perspective 5. High stakes
Prepare for Develop Events	Simulate Determine Events	Evaluate Determine Events
Not in Gradebook	*In Gradebook but Inactive*	*In Gradebook and Active*

Source: Reibel, 2018b.

Deliver	Develop	Determine
Homework 1	Quiz 2	Quiz 4
Quiz 1	Quiz 3	Test 1
Group activity 2	Project 1	Warm up 1
Video activity 1	Class discussion 1	Homework 2
Exit activity 1	Test 2	Group activity 1

Figure 3.3: Assessment purposes inventory.

Remember that instruction and assessment must occupy the same pedagogical space for proficiency-based learning to function properly. In each lesson, the teacher chooses to deploy one of these event types (deliver, develop, determine) with each student as he or she produces evidence of competence. When teachers see instruction and assessment as occupying the same pedagogical space, they can consider a lesson nothing more than an evidence-based conversation about learning. Embracing this idea is critical when planning proficiency-based lessons.

Question 2: What Is the Role of a Standard or Learning Target?

In many schools, the principal expects teachers to post their standards and learning targets on the whiteboard each day in class. While this is not a bad idea, there is not a whole lot to be gained by simply posting the standards and targets on the board. Standards and targets have a more central role in proficiency-based instruction.

Standards and learning targets are an active pedagogical element to be mobilized in instruction, not a static element used only for communicating what content to teach that day in class. Targets act as expectations of competency and proficiency that engage students by tapping into factors which stimulate reflection, heighten a focus on one's own thinking, and set the stage for feedback acceptance.

Following are five ways teachers can mobilize a target in their instruction.

1. **Use targets as a *benchmark* of learning:** In order to self-navigate, students need a clear destination for their learning. They need more than just model exemplars; they need to know what proficiency actually is. When you offer students clear expectations for learning, you create a classroom culture where they can self-regulate their own growth.

2. **Use targets to outline expected proficiency:** Make regular statements about the expected proficiency of any given target and relate it to student thinking. Whenever there is an opportunity to connect what a student has produced to the target's proficiency expectation, do so.

3. **Use targets to give purpose to the activities in the lesson:** Targets should provide direction for both teachers and students. Students should not just see the target on the board but the layout of the lesson and how it relates to targeted expectations prior to starting each day. Visually represent the connections between the students, new learning, and the proficiency aspects of the target. For example, you might explain why learning about data analysis is important. In the lesson, you might visually represent the consequences of misreading data by identifying historic examples of scientific blunders, miscalculated political decisions, or misreading of data that led to political errors. By supporting learning targets with purposeful reasons to learn, students come to recognize why developing proficiency has significance.

4. **Use targets to react to students' learning needs:** Targets allow the teacher to pivot in the direction students need during the lesson. By using student evidence and a variety of assessments, the teacher can interweave different activities and react to students in

order to offer appropriate solutions. Gather evidence of how well a student is developing a skill throughout a lesson, which provides the information necessary to change instructional approaches, if needed. For example, during reading instruction, you might discover that a student needs more specific, guided questions to help direct him or her to key details; or, alternatively, provide an advanced reader with more challenging questions focused on higher-order critical-thinking skills.

5. **Use target language as your script for feedback:** Targets allow students to reflect on their learning more easily. *Asking* students to self-assess their proficiency is more effective feedback than *telling* students where they are. Likewise, self-reported evaluation provides other insights regarding students' self-awareness. For example, if you ask students to describe how they performed on a mathematics exam—where they did well and where they might have struggled—they begin to gain more confidence in what they know and material they need to review to gain greater confidence in their own developing proficiencies.

Targets are an important pedagogical tool for promoting self-realization, self-monitoring, and self-awareness in each student, and they are an essential component in proficiency-based instruction.

Question 3: Should My Classroom Be Content Focused or Competency Focused?

A competency focus is different than a content focus. When we refer to *content*, we are generally talking about what a student needs to know in order to perform a competency. When we refer to *competency*, we are generally talking about how capable a student is at understanding or performing content or skills, which is the same as proficiency. Why is this an important distinction? In proficiency-based instruction the classroom should always focus on competency, as competence breeds confidence, which leads to self-regulated learning and growth (or efficacy).

Sadly, content-focused teaching and learning is common practice in education. Many schools see familiarity with content as competence. However, since students are only shallowly engaging with the material, it takes more repetition and practice, sometimes called *massed practice* (Brown et al., 2014), to retain it just long enough for the pending assessment. With this learning focus, students are simply "renting" knowledge (Guo, 2015).

Renting is the idea that students become familiar with the content or skill in a course until the rental period is over (the test). It may appear that the student has mastered the skill or content but in reality, has only retained it in his or her short-term memory and capabilities (Guo, 2015). Short-term memory involves recall of information for a relatively short period of time. In *Make It Stick*, Brown et al. (2014) state that learning moves from short-term to long-term memory, memory that involves the storage and recall of information over a long period of time, when students are asked to engage in something they call "retrieval" (p. 75).

Creating events that demand retrieval of certain knowledge and skills from previous experiences consolidates learning and increases the likelihood that it enters long-term memory (Brown et al., 2014). The problem is that these renting instructional models are based on short-term activities and are not structured to have students retrieve learning from prior experiences.

Short-term production can appear as mastery because many current lessons don't scrutinize student thinking as they should. Verifying each and every aspect of a unit's content before a student attempts the targeted proficiency expectation not only is inefficient but creates a false sense of learning. Brown et al. (2014) relate that it gives students a "warm sensation of mastery because they are looping information through short-term memory without having to reconstruct the learning from long term memory" (p. 82).

However, in a competency-focused lesson, the performance and development of student proficiency are the main goals of each lesson. Teachers review and teach content only after students have experienced the competency. In his book *Brilliant Mistakes,* Paul J. H. Schoemaker (2011) discusses the idea of competency-focused classrooms:

> While [students] can often learn faster by making more mistakes, it's also fair to acknowledge that *learning* is not always the most important goal. There are critical moments, and specific tasks, where high performance should and will be [the] only concern. (p. 169)

Teachers should design proficiency-based lessons with this in mind. Lessons focus on developing proficiency. Students should learn content, concepts, or strategies while they are developing proficiency, not before.

Question 4: What Is an Anticipatory Set, and What Does It Look Like in Proficiency-Based Instruction?

Jennifer Gonzalez (2014) states the time-honored definition of an anticipatory set in this way: "A brief portion of a lesson given at the very beginning to get students' attention, activate prior knowledge, and prepare them for the day's learning. Also known as *advance organizer, hook*, or *set induction*."

While an anticipatory set is important, we see a significantly different purpose. In proficiency-based instruction, teachers use the anticipatory set to allow students to perform a *prelesson self-calibration* against the desired state of proficiency. In other words, teachers do not use the anticipatory set to prepare students for the lesson; they use it to capture and reflect on each student's initial state of proficiency. The resulting information creates the *foundation* for the rest of the lesson, as it creates a touchpoint to which the teacher can relate all subsequent learning during the lesson. So, teachers can use the anticipatory set as an initial proficiency performance. This is essential for proficiency-based instruction and grading.

Without this initial self-discovery and reflection on proficiency, learning typically defaults to the rote acquisition or performance of skills and content. It serves students better if teachers spend the majority of their time in development with students, providing them with the critical, yet low-stakes feedback about their progress with the standards and learning targets. The feedback from this development is much less threatening to students and is more readily accepted and used.

Regardless of how we view learning, the fact remains that instruction is more reaction than delivery—student to teacher and teacher to student—and teachers should strive to design lessons that engage students in competency experiences to effectively support them in their learning.

Key Takeaways From Chapter 3

Review these key points with your team to reinforce the concepts from this chapter.

1. There are three major uses for assessment within a proficiency-based instructional model: deliver, develop, and determine. In sum, focus on delivering the supporting and prerequisite skills for further learning. Lessons should focus on developing proficiencies for all students based on set, clear expectations and, ultimately, evaluation.

2. Learning targets have five purposes: (1) to serve as a benchmark; (2) to set clear expectations for proficiency; (3) to give purpose to the lesson; (4) to provide a clear focus for reacting to student learning; and (5) to direct the language needed for feedback.

3. Teachers should focus lessons on developing the competency of student skills.

4. Quickly assessing every student's proficiency level is central to beginning the lesson in a proficiency-based classroom. These quick assessments help to position the starting point for learning during the lesson.

Stop, Think, Reflect

With your team, reflect on the following three questions to continue with the collaborative process for change.

1. In what ways has your team collaborated to write learning targets that are informative, clear, and focused on proficiency expectations for all learners?

2. As your team collaborates to implement proficiency-based instruction, in what ways can you compare and contrast the value of student learning experiences so you can better consider approaches to teaching and learning?

3. In what ways does proficiency-based instruction help generate conversations around interventions?

Insight

In chapter 4, we focus on the many important insights that accompany the shift to proficiency-based instruction. As teachers become more familiar with the changes of lesson design and delivery and spend time implementing them, aha moments begin to occur. Valuable insights emerge that profoundly affect teachers' instruction and students' learning. As with any change, it is important for teachers and leaders to guide and discuss the change while it is happening. These collaborative debriefings allow team-structured time to identify what is working and what might need more support. They also allow teachers to share their insights about teaching and learning and specifically identify why the shift to a proficiency-based instructional model works to support and develop every student's potential.

Following are four key points to remember during the insight stage.

1. Not all instructional choices make an impact on learning. Some instructional choices may even be counterproductive to learning.

2. Instructional practices focused on developing proficiency create a classroom structure that provides immediate feedback on student learning and generates real-time instructional shifts to support student growth.

3. Higher functioning teams develop insights into better instructional practices when they spend time collaborating during the formative development of student learning.

4. Collaborating to analyze and create instructional insights helps teams reach all students.

Teaching and learning are about creating moments of insight, times when we can say to ourselves, "Aha!" Suddenly, we make sense of something.

Making the shifts necessary for proficiency-based instruction requires a number of aha moments. Four overriding insights guide changes to proficiency-based instruction: (1) making an impact on every student; (2) making immediate, real-time changes in teaching and learning practices; (3) relying on collaborative teaming structures; and (4) inquiring for continuous improvement.

The teaming process nurtures developing, collaborative insights. When we are in collaborative conversations with other experts, we fuel one another's thinking and we begin to see problems in new ways. In doing this, solutions begin to emerge that can affect all students. A shift to proficiency-based instruction is a commitment to implement current research practices that better inform teaching and learning.

As we work toward this model in which we constantly monitor student growth in real time, we must commit to recognizing that certain teaching and learning practices are more effective than others and—perhaps more important—that certain traditional practices are ineffective or even counterproductive to learning, such as content-focused rubrics, activities that promote mimicry, and assessments that primary rely on recall. A proficiency-based classroom monitors learning growth in real time, and the effort fosters a commitment to immediate instructional changes that promote immediate growth. These insights into teaching and learning align with strong formative assessment models, which recognize that teachers and students need to create or seek corrective feedback *as learning is developing*, not after a summative assessment event, the end of a unit, or the end of a semester or year. Looking back on teaching and learning concerns does not help foster growth as a day-to-day commitment.

As you read our team's story, pay attention to how insights related to proficiency-based instruction emerge, and keep these three things in mind.

1. Consider how the team embraces the instructional planning template designed to deliberately develop proficiency.

2. Consider that the team plans its lessons with *student does* first instead of *teacher models* first.

3. Consider how the team discusses the importance of reperformance and reflection in the proficiency-based instructional model.

Our Team's Story

Early in the year, Marcos set up collaborative meetings in which the team could discuss how proficiency-based instruction created an impact on student learning. During the incubation stage, the team agreed on a strong *why* behind a shift away from traditional instructional models. Now the team could focus on how well the change helped the students. Team members continued their team meetings, at this point discussing their developing insights. Team members focused on the role instruction played in their assessment practices and the results they were seeing in student growth.

Marcos was really excited about his team meetings. The team was moving beyond the coordinating, calendaring, and sharing of lessons. From his personal experience, he felt like the shift to a proficiency-based instructional model allowed students to experience competency in a deeper way than in previous years, and he recognized that he was learning more from his colleagues and helping students more quickly. The team was finally examining student results as they were developing day by day and week by week.

Marcos opened the next meeting with excitement. He said, "I know we are all making some significant shifts in our lesson planning. Over the last few weeks, we've been sharing our insights daily and during team meetings. At this point, I think we might want to really check in and identify some of the patterns we are seeing in our students and in our instructional efforts to make the shift to proficiency-based instruction. What do you view to be some of our strengths, and what do we think are some areas we might need to work on?"

Marcos continued, "As we discuss our insights, let's be sure to review a few of our norms. First, remember that we are here to critique ideas and support innovations. This is a big change, so it is really important for everyone to give input openly and honestly. Second, let's be sure to keep an open mind. We can really help students if we maintain our willingness to try new ideas and listen to diverse opinions."

Tony said, "Nico and I talked several times over the last week. I think we both felt that this structure helped us to focus on students' formative development. In our lessons, we noticed that we were paying closer attention to individual student development and progressing each learner. I'm starting to get a much better understanding of why and how we can use formative assessment practices, and I think I'm looking at differentiated instruction in an entirely different way."

"I agree," Nico added. "The proficiency-based instructional model reminds me that every lesson should work to progress every student. Our previous instructional approach helped a percentage of students develop, but a focus on developing proficiency reminds me that every student is developing his or her learning from different starting points, and it builds off the understanding that learning develops at different paces. The proficiency-based instructional model also helps students realize they need to take owner-ship of their learning. Every day for the past two weeks, I've asked them to report back on their own perceptions of their learning. That offered me a lot of insights into, for example, students' confidence levels, students hyper-focusing on certain aspects of the concept, or students not using the most efficient way to solve a problem. I think my students are getting better at identifying what they know and what they still need to improve."

Tony commented, "Yes, and I think we are both seeing a big improvement in our students' finished work. Since we are building off our work with for-mative assessments, we are providing better feedback to students along the way. By the end of the week and our first unit, there was definitely evidence of learning developing over time."

Sofie and Lauren nodded, and Sofie said, "Yes, definitely, Nico and Tony. My conversations with students are much richer now, too. They are getting better at discussing the skills they are learning and starting to understand that learning skills *develop over time*. In the past, I think my students thought they needed to just learn something once, and then they could do it. This year, I think they are realizing that they need to learn new skills and con-tinue to develop those skills. My students are starting to understand the pro-cess of growth. They are recognizing that lessons are designed to challenge everyone to reach their own greatest potential. It is a very different mindset for my students. One student had been struggling at the beginning of the week, and on Thursday she said, 'So, it seems like you aren't going to give up on me until I can do this.' This was really different from how my students viewed lessons before."

Lauren said, "In talking with Tony this week, we noticed that students are seeing the writing process as being about continuous improvement. We've been spending more time talking about developing different writing compe-tencies, and students are starting to have stronger conversations with their peers about each other's writing. They are getting better at evaluating one another's skills and offering suggestions to each other during the reflection process. During my lessons, I've structured more time to nurture higher levels of collaboration. Since students are getting better at discussing proficiency-based skills, they are getting better at working within their groups. It's been pretty exciting."

Marcos agreed and said that his experience was the same in that students were much more aware of what was expected of them before they even got to the final essay.

"Right," Tony said. "I think students are catching on that our work together is to nurture growth over time, and they see each lesson like a series of scrimmages in order to improve. By the time they are ready to submit evidence of their performance, they know that they are prepared and are clear on our course expectations."

Nico added, "While I like this new format for unit planning, I still feel like something during the lesson isn't aligned properly for my students, and I might need some help. I mean, I still rely on my warm-up activities to engage students, and I tend to find myself falling back into my traditional habits for teaching. After the opening activity, they work in small groups or individually and practice. Then they complete an exit slip. I don't feel like I'm working with the structure as effectively as I could be. My teaching just seems linear."

Marcos said, "I understand what you are getting at, Nico. I think the big shift came when I realized that our traditional model of 'gradual release' didn't fit within the proficiency-based instructional model. Actually, that linear idea of *I do, we do, you do* is what we really need to change. In some ways, we need to break that habit and think very differently."

Lauren said, "For instance, the other day instead of a warm-up, I had students immediately write a short argument to their previous classroom teacher about why they shouldn't have received homework that night. Then I simply used that paragraph as teaching material for the rest of the class. Students took the components of good writing and reviewed the short paragraph to see if they made a valid argument or not. As the conversation expanded, I used feedback from students about their own work to guide my lesson as a model. That is very different from starting with me modeling. Instead, I started with their work. The learning experience became much more authentic for students, and their work became the starting point of the lesson. As the class continued, students were better able to compare and contrast their writing and identify individual areas for growth."

Marcos summarized, "So, I like what you are saying. It sounds like you started with *you do* instead of *I do*. There was no gradual release. It sounds like it was immediate release."

Tony pondered this for a moment and said, "I guess you're right. I think Lauren just changed decades of education practice. I mean, sometimes we need to show first, but I think what we need to recognize is that we really need to start with students' work first before we assume what they need to learn."

This idea started to challenge the team. They thought more about the entrenched ideas of how they had traditionally designed and implemented lessons.

Sofie said, "I think we are going to generate a lot of different insights in the next few months. Breaking away from the gradual release model is a very significant shift, and I think it is a pretty important change to monitor. I don't want us to walk away thinking that we don't still need to model changes in learning for students. At times, that is still necessary, right?"

Nico said, "Yes, like when you have to model the application of Newton's first law of motion, introduce a new aspect of the quadratic formula, or explain how to augment a thesis statement. But ultimately, these should be small parts of our lessons."

Marcos said, "Yes, I agree. It's like all the things we talked about before, too. I think the important point to remember is that we need to begin our lessons with the learners in mind first. If we aren't doing that, we are off track."

Tony said, "OK, let's try to sum this up and see if we understand this correctly. Before, we assumed all students started the class below competency, and our job was to model for them and then move them to competency. We used the *I do, we do, you do* gradual release of responsibility model to manage how we sequenced activities. For example, we would show our students an example of good writing and teach them about all the small components of writing an argument. However, with proficiency-based instruction, we want to invert that process. Instead, the student starts the lesson, and then the class, and then the teacher works to model new learning and reinforce or challenge students in ways that extend learning. So, our graph begins to look like this." Tony drew a diagram on the board (see figure 4.1).

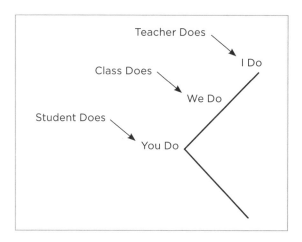

Figure 4.1: First stage of a proficiency-based lesson plan—Student-first model.

Nico said, "I think Sofie's and Lauren's comments really stress that shift, and it sounds like they have made some really great revisions to how they are designing their lessons."

Marcos continued, "At this point, I think we want to pay closer attention to the second half of the diagram, the portion that is halfway through the lesson. This is when the class works together again, and then it goes back to the individual student."

"Yes, this is exactly how Sofie and I were thinking the other day," Tony said. "If we were to add to the diagram, it would look more like this." He continued to draw on the board, adding a second triangle, creating a diamond (see figure 4.2).

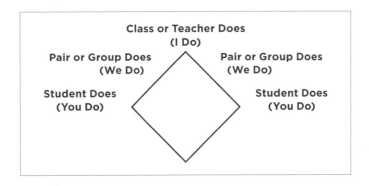

Figure 4.2: Instructional diamond lesson plan—Student-first model.

Tony noted, "Hey, it looks like a diamond! It helps me visualize how I should structure lessons in my class. I can simply plan to open and then close the diamond."

Nico added, "Catchy name, the *instructional diamond*. I like it!"

Sofie said, "Yes, agreed. I guess I have been applying this instructional diamond already. The important thing I'm noticing is that after I spend time working with students to progress their learning, they need to spend time working with one another to reinforce and process new learning in their collaborative groups. This diamond lesson design is really valuable because it helps to extend thinking and pace the learning among different students."

"I like what Sofie just said," Lauren added. "One important point for me is that when I'm working with students' collaborative groups, I provide different feedback for each student that helps to guide and develop his or her individual growth. The instructional diamond reminds me of the importance of that effort, and what I'm noticing is really interesting. The individual feedback I'm giving to students during the first half of the lesson guides the feedback students will give each other during the second part of the lesson when we ask them to work collaboratively again."

Nico said, "So, the feedback you give continues to radiate throughout the room during the class period. Students develop in how they comment and evaluate one another's work during peer-to-peer feedback."

"Yes," Marcos agreed. "I think that is one of the more important features of the work we are doing. I talked with some of the mathematics teachers, and they said the same thing. Their students are getting better at working together because they develop a stronger ability to comment on one another's thinking and problem solving."

Lauren added, "I like the diamond template for other reasons, too. I don't want us to forget that students need to be continuously self-assessing during this process. So, as we are thinking about the diamond, the real value is when students develop a clearer understanding of their own reflective judgment."

Marcos noticed that their collaborative time was ending and said, "Thank you. I think that was a really strong meeting filled with some thoughtful insights. This week, let's really commit to working on this diamond-shaped template for our lesson design. I think the design helps us interconnect more about how we want to teach and how we can work to create effective instructional practices for our students."

Two Insights of Proficiency-Based Instruction

In the journey toward proficiency-based instruction, there are two key insights teachers have related to lesson design and delivery.

1. Proficiency-based instructional design begins and ends with student performance.

2. Lessons should close by building efficacy and self-reliance.

Insight 1: Proficiency-Based Instructional Design Begins and Ends With Student Performance

Proficiency-based instruction should always begin and end with a focus on the students and what they are *doing*. When teachers design lessons to begin and end with what the student *does*, the learning experience becomes more generative and personalized.

As proficiency-based teachers, we must understand that a significant aspect of our role is to help students develop a sense of efficacy. To do this, we must embrace the idea that we do not judge student performance through a process of verification or testing knowledge and skills but instead through a reflective process in which evidence and experience contextualize and ultimately validate that performance (Gobble et al., 2016). The practice of proficiency-based teaching develops a student's reflective capacity while ensuring the student's accumulated knowledge. This type of practice is predicated on a commitment to the following instructional mantra: "I don't care what I think about your learning, I care what you think about your learning" (Elbaum, 2015, p. 4).

To some teachers, the statement may initially seem confusing, and they might ask themselves the following questions.

▸ "Wait, why would I not evaluate a student's level of knowledge or skill?"

▸ "Shouldn't I care about student achievement?"

▸ "If I don't care about their learning, how will I give grades?"

While these are legitimate questions, if they are the first questions we attempt to answer, we have lost sight of our true role as facilitators of meaningful, proficiency-based learning.

We suggest that teachers implement proficiency-based instruction through the following four-step framework.

1. **Personalize the proficiency (individual):** Proficiency-based teachers create a classroom environment in which students learn how to privately scrutinize and question their level of proficiency. Making students aware of their competency levels is essential at this stage.

2. **Scrutinize the proficiency (pairs and small groups):** Proficiency-based teachers create a classroom environment in which students can engage in reflective conversations as they further scrutinize and question their level of proficiency.

3. **Verify the proficiency (whole class):** Proficiency-based teachers create a classroom environment in which students work interdependently with other students and their teacher to further develop their level of proficiency.

4. **Repeat steps 1 and 2:** Proficiency-based teachers realize the importance of reperformance. Teachers should offer students a chance to use feedback to expand, reshape, change, or reflect on their initial performance or attempt.

Together, these four steps ensure that all proficiency-based lessons succeed and entrench long-term practice. To help visualize this framework, think about a diamond. A diamond has two primary points, is made up of two triangles, and has a wide middle section. This is an effective metaphor for how we should consider teaching.

If we apply the proficiency-based teaching framework, keeping this shape in mind, we see an effective balance of individual reflection, consensus and sense making, and perspective creating. Let's take a closer look at this framework, as shown in figure 4.3. By working through the diamond lesson plan, students can make better sense of their learning, have a more realistic perspective of self, enhance their reflection skills, and come to consensus with others about what they are learning.

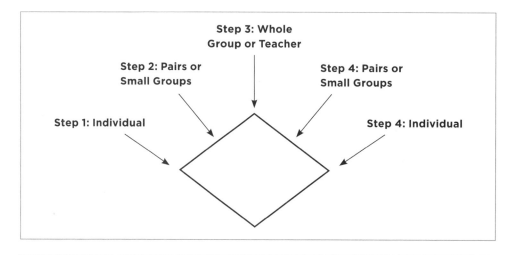

Figure 4.3: Instructional diamond lesson structure.

Following are the four steps of the instructional diamond framework.

1. **Personalize the learning (individual):** This is when learners privately scrutinize their own state of proficiency.

2. **Scrutinize the learning (pairs or small groups):** This is when learners engage in reflective dialogue with a variety of peers within multiple contexts (pairs and small groups) to properly scrutinize their level of proficiency.

3. **Concretize the learning (whole group or teacher):** This is when learners collaboratively vet and further develop their proficiency levels through the guidance of the whole class, including all of its resources. This is where learners garner an accurate perspective of themselves, their growth, and their abilities.

4. **Elaborate the learning (pairs or small groups or individual):** This is when learners engage in individual adjustments or elaborations to their newly consolidated learning or skill. This backside of the diamond is for reshaping, adding, subtracting, and molding their proficiency. This is essential for helping learners apply feedback, envision growth, and refine their proficiency.

Personalize the Learning (Individual)

We know it's important for students to personalize learning in the classroom. What is not as clear is how to make that happen. It's not enough for students to simply work on tasks and problems in personalized situations. They must capture a current state of proficiency and immediately connect it to a learning target that makes sense to them.

This initial self-calibration of proficiency provides students a context for their individual abilities and provides a guidepost for the rest of their learning. In other words, this current-state self-assessment gives students insight into what proficiency is and what trajectory of growth they are on. Engaging students in self-evaluating their proficiency level first creates a personalized framework from which they learn, making them feel more invested in their own learning.

In this step, teachers engage students in activities that allow for self-reflection, contemplation, and self-assessment of where they are in relation to the competencies of the course. Here students make sure they've identified what it is that they are expected to know, understand, or do. This step offers activities that allow students to experience the expected competency in individual and highly personalized ways with no consequences for their grades. The purpose of this crucial step of instruction is to capture a current state of competency from which all subsequent learning relates as the lesson or unit progresses. Students must be able to state very clearly an accurate picture of their learning and use any and all evidence to support this perspective.

Proficiency-based teachers create a classroom environment in which students learn how to *privately* scrutinize and self-question their level of proficiency. They engage in internal rhetoric regarding their own state of learning and thinking. To put it simply, we want students in this step to gather evidence and think about it through self-reflection.

In step 1, proficiency-based teachers understand that instead of only assessing answers or outcomes, they must also assess students' ability to articulate and scrutinize the evidence of their current state of proficiency. This skill is important to developing an accurate perspective of one's own learning, which is essential for an effective learning experience. If you don't have the correct learning perspective, it might lead to overconfidence, insecurity, and confusion. Ultimately, lasting learning will have less potential to occur.

Teachers must use the information that students produce during these individual reflective experiences in step 1 to properly assess and instruct. These reflection data give a teacher valuable information and insight into how students are *attempting* to learn the material, which is a different perspective from *if* they learned the material.

Teachers must possess the ability to actively listen for evidence of these attempts and use this material to teach. Furthermore, getting students to scrutinize and articulate the patterns they see in their work helps teachers access the *attempting to learn* data that are so important for learning. This is the important stuff! Think about it this way: if teachers simply judge students on how they learn the material, that would be like a basketball coach judging his or her team's performance solely on whether the ball goes through the hoop. We all know this is an inaccurate way to coach, and the same applies to teaching; a teacher should not base his or her instruction and assessment decisions solely on the mastery outcomes. Teachers must include the perspectives students have about their own learning, which includes information students provide as they articulate how they perceive their current state of proficiency.

During step 1, getting students to contemplate their unclassified (ungraded, unscored, or not evaluated) state of learning is essential. To contemplate effectively, students must do two things: (1) self-assess and (2) self-evaluate. You may be thinking, Aren't these terms the same? In proficiency-based teaching, they are two different experiences, as Kathleen Gregory, Caren Cameron, and Anne Davies (2011) outline in the book *Self-Assessment and Goal Setting*. The authors state that these two entities are different experiences: "Assessment involves collecting information on student performance; evaluation involves examining all of the assessment data and then making judgments about individual performance" (Gregory et al., 2011, p. 60).

One method for having students examine their state of learning is through interaction with a proficiency-based target. As we stated earlier, proficiency-based targets are a gradation of competency levels acting as a learning outcome (Gobble et al., 2016). See an example of a fourth-grade geography proficiency-based scale in figure 4.4.

---

4 Beyond proficient (exceeds mastery)—<u>Use maps of different scales</u> to describe locations of <u>different</u> cultural and environmental characteristics.

3 Proficient (mastery)—<u>Use maps of different scales</u> to describe the locations of <u>similar</u> cultural and environmental characteristics.

2 Developing proficiency (emerging)—<u>Use maps of the same scale</u> to describe the locations of <u>similar</u> cultural and environmental characteristics.

1 Foundational skills (still developing)—<u>Use a map</u> to describe the locations of <u>similar</u> cultural and environmental characteristics.

Figure 4.4: Scaled proficiency targets for fourth-grade geography.

In the self-assessment part of this first step, students can act as archaeologists of sorts, unearthing patterns in their evidence, connecting details, and beginning inquiry into their work that relates to the proficiency-based target. The key here is that students must disregard, consider irrelevant, and discard any evidence that doesn't relate to a proficiency-based target.

When students go through the process of deciding what information and evidence are relevant to the expectation before them, it promotes and expedites learning. This means that the teacher must provide time for students to review their unclassified work. The student must then take his or her evidence and relate it to the language of the proficiency-based target, not a grade or score. In the self-assessment part of contemplating students, don't use the full scale just yet.

First, use the language in the proficient level of this target, level 3: "Use maps of different scales to describe the locations of similar cultural and environmental characteristics." Once students have uncovered enough evidence, in their perspective, they must move to the second part of contemplation: self-evaluation. As stated previously, self-evaluation is the independent judgment of one's evidence uncovered during the self-assessment process. To do this properly, students now use the full scale in figure 4.4, along with reflective guidance from the teacher, to help judge their current state of competency. Reflective guidance might include the teacher asking questions like the following.

- ▸ "Where would you place yourself?"
- ▸ "What evidence is leading you to that rank?"
- ▸ "Were there any patterns in the evidence that surprised you?"
- ▸ "What in your evidence would you identify as strengths?"

Once students have gathered the evidence (self-assessment) and ranked themselves (self-evaluation), they can now develop the skill of self-questioning. Doug Buehl (2011) states that self-questioning is the ability to pose questions "while engaged in making sense" or learning (p. 171). This is exactly what this step of proficiency-based teaching demands of students—scrutinizing their current state of learning. Stated differently, students scrutinize where they are in relation to the target.

To aid in this, teachers must create reflective experiences based on questions such as, What evidence might be missing at this point? Did you leave anything out? What if I told you that this aspect of the learning target is more essential to your learning? Or, you can think about it this way: teachers should use a technique similar to the one an eye doctor uses to evaluate your vision. During a typical eye exam, the doctor asks you to read a line of letters. After you do that, the doctor does not say you're right or wrong but flips to a new lens type and asks, "How about now? Clearer? Worse?"

Experiences like this can help students decipher the quality of their work and, more importantly, determine whether they have an accurate perspective of their work. Buehl (2011) outlines a taxonomy for self-questioning that proves beneficial for developing these types of dissecting questions. We have adapted it in table 4.1 to relate it to proficiency-based teaching.

Table 4.1: Proficiency-Based Self-Inquiry (Step 1)

Level of Thinking	Comprehension Process	Self-Inquiry Questions
Creating	Synthesizing Creating mental imagery	As I review my work, is any new knowledge emerging?
Evaluating	Inferring	What is the message I am getting about my own proficiency from my work?
Analyzing	Making connections Determining importance	Are there clear patterns of proficiency in my work? Where?
Applying	Making connections Inferring	What is my work making me think now?
Understanding	Determining importance Inferring Creating mental models	What are strengths and weaknesses in my work?
Remembering	Determining importance Creating mental models	What is the most important part of my work?

It is essential that teachers create these types of learning spaces in step 1 so students can engage with these questions in an act of private deliberation, pattern recognition, and self-inquiry. The ability to self-question in regard to one's own proficiency is not only a prerequisite skill for step 2 but also an essential skill for developing self-awareness and self-reliance.

Becoming a proficiency-based teacher means learning how to create learning experiences that expose *how students are attempting* to learn instead of experiences that expose *if they learned*. There are three ways to create individual-focused learning experiences.

1. Outline expected competency and criteria.

2. Capture a current state of understanding or skill.

3. Create desirably difficult situations.

Outline Expected Competency and Criteria

At the very beginning of a lesson, a student must understand and be able to visualize the expected competency level and the associated criteria. This means that a lesson, at its onset, must outline an answer to one very specific question: How well do I need to demonstrate the skill or understanding we are about to experience? Lessons must strive to develop *full competence,* a fully rooted state of competence, of each skill they outline. Often, teachers build lessons toward *acceptable competence*, which is an illusionary state of rooted competence but is still just temporary and shallow skill demonstration. For example, a mathematics teacher might help students understand full competence of graphing a polynomial by saying it is "graphing a polynomial in an *unfamiliar context with the essential components.*"

Planning toward expected competence may create a more rigorous learning environment that contributes to some initial anxiety in learning for both the student and teacher. However, in the long run the anxiety will subside, and competence and efficacy will take its place. This is where the learning target or standard is essential.

Learning targets commonly serve as thematic guideposts for student learning, outlining the topics and granular concepts covered by instruction. They are essentially a long list of things to learn.

These targets are also statements of expected competency. Targets are mechanisms that help contextualize one's learning and provide a perspective on *how well* one is actually doing. This perspective helps drive students' reflection abilities, self-awareness, and perspective of their learning. When students use learning targets as statements of the expected state of competence, they exhibit a growth mindset and see learning as navigating the targets' outlined expectation of proficiency.

Capture a Current State of Understanding or Skill

Immediately at the onset of the lesson, it is important pedagogically to capture a current state of understanding from each student, and then work with this state. Gaining this understanding yields fertile ground for personalizing learning and creating competency. When you work with each student's current thinking, skill level, and knowledge, students have a higher chance of accepting any feedback, applying it, and growing from it.

If you ask students to constantly reflect on their current state of learning as the central activity of proficiency-based instruction, then they have no choice but to actively engage in their learning. This is because the lesson relies on them having a current state to work from. Without a current state of learning, students cannot proceed through the lesson. Also, when students are working with something as highly personal as their current state of learning, they are motivated to accept feedback more readily, work with it, and see their state of learning grow.

Students must be the center of instruction, as instruction is a reaction to student-produced evidence. This means that if students are reflectively engaged with a learning target to produce evidence, the teacher should simply pause until the reflection is over, let students articulate their thoughts and learning connections, and then react (move the instruction) to students' responses.

Create Desirably Difficult Situations

The idea of errorless learning outlined by B. F. Skinner promotes spoon-fed instruction of material and assessment of learning that focuses on immediate and short-term memory (Brown et al., 2014). In proficiency-based instruction, teachers must resist creating lessons that spoon-feed the material. Rather, they must embrace pausing, creating reflective spacing, adding nuance, and adding twists in contexts to create learning experiences that are what Brown et al. (2014) call "desirably difficult." This means keeping the proficiency and rigor of learning at the exact cognitive position that students have to reach for but can still achieve . . . if they apply a level of cognitive effort.

The problem is that desirably difficult lessons are hard to preplan because they rely on reacting to in-the-moment student thinking while still maintaining the right level of rigor. Therefore, teachers must create desirably difficult lessons dynamically, on the spot, as students provide evidence of where they are and where they are going. This student-produced evidence determines what is the desirable difficulty level of the lesson, and the teacher must know how to recognize it and use it effectively.

To show how desirably difficult lessons work, let's return to the eye exam analogy. When the eye doctor examines your eyes, he does not predetermine what lenses to give you; he listens to your responses as you read each line of letters, changes the lenses, and then asks, "What do you see now?" Teachers must do the same thing with proficiency-based instruction to capture current states of learning. They can do this by using a *how about now* approach to teaching. In this approach, teachers constantly provide new lenses for students to view their work with the material.

Charlotte Danielson (2007) calls on educators to do the same thing using her teaching rubric: "The teacher persists in seeking effective approaches for students who need help, using an extensive repertoire of instructional strategies and soliciting additional resources from the school" (p. 91).

Danielson (2009) further challenges us to rely on vast knowledge of instructional strategies as we react to student evidence.

This evidence-based, desirably difficult instruction causes the right learning to occur. What is the right learning in proficiency-based instruction? As Brown et al. (2014) state, the spaced pausing of variable segments of learning promotes "skills of discrimination—the process of noticing particulars . . . and of induction: surmising the general rule" (p. 84). Skills of discrimination are key to distinguishing one's own level of expertise (current state of learning), which is essential to active participation in learning.

Scrutinize the Learning (Pairs or Small Groups)

It is not enough to simply work in groups; in proficiency-based instruction, students must work in groups to compare and scrutinize their current state of proficiency with others' to gain context and a sense of reality of their own abilities and understanding. Without the opportunity to scrutinize their conceptions and abilities with others in a nonevaluative way, students won't have the potential to fully develop proficiency.

Step 2 is about engaging with peers to create the correct learning perspective so students can build future learning on solid mental maps and understanding. When students vet their current state of learning publicly, we see a higher rate of retention and an increase in student engagement.

During this step, it is important for students to compare and contrast competencies with others without any learning consequence. Teachers should know how to create activities that allow students to have open, safe, dissonant conversations about the realities of their competencies and how they relate to the expectations for the course. In this step, the teacher must model safe and mature methods for students to critically analyze their current state of competency. This step asks students to review their competencies honestly and openly with classmates. The activities in this step must promote self-regulation, self-monitoring, and critical and honest evaluation of one's current state of competency. Here the teacher acts as a mediator between students, maybe for the first time, and engages in the reality of competency development.

Being a proficiency-based teacher means allowing students to engage in reflective dialogue in order to explore and revise their thoughts and possibly analyze those thoughts publicly. These conversations are not only difficult but require a lot of cognitive stamina to perform. However difficult, these conversations are the centerpiece of this step in the process. It is essential that the teacher promotes active inquiry.

Whereas in step 1 students learned to question their state of learning privately, in step 2, they must learn to question publicly and engage in transparent reflective dialogue about their current state of learning. Teachers can help students do this by doing the following.

▸ **Inviting students to use nonevaluative langauge when self-appraising their work with others:** When we ask students to self-evaluate, it helps build their efficacy to also do this in front of others. Students can consolidate their thoughts about their own proficiency, which helps create an accurate perspective. Teachers can help students do this by reminding them to avoid comments like, "I think I made a well-crafted argument because . . ." or "My argument was not that great because I forgot to add . . ." But rather, teachers should invite students to say comments such as, "I did this because this is what quality arguments have" or "From what I understand, good arguments have these characteristics." The shift in language is essential because it helps students see their work as a product of their skills and not a representation of self. This separation helps students see their work objectively and increases the chance of meaningful and honest self-evaluation.

▸ **Inviting students to use nonevaluative language when critiquing a peer's work:** When students engage in learning conversations with each other, it is usually evaluative, stating things like, "This was a good part. You did this well. You didn't use the required [item]." Helping students interact in a nonevaluative manner can lead to better reflective conversations that maximize learning in the moment. For example, students engaged in a nonevaluative conversation might say, "What are you attempting to say here? Would you say this segment is proficient? If you had to do this section again, what would you add or change?" This type of conversation keeps reflective accountability on the producer of the work but more importantly, lets him or her evaluate him or herself. The peer in this case is simply a mechanism creating self-evaluation. Accurate self-evaluation is essential to efficacy (Bandura, 1997).

▸ **Inviting students to use nonevaluative language when consulting with the teacher:** Typically, students interact with their teacher or evaluator by discussing the evaluation. When students focus on the evaluation score in their discussions with the teacher, the conversations become reductive, meaning they become simply about the grade. Students engaged in an evaluative conversation with their teacher might sound like, "Well you got three points for [this], and then I took off a point here because you didn't add [that]. You got four points here because you added [this component]." This creates dialogue that is more deficiency-based and procedural.

However, a student engaged in a nonevaluative discussion with a teacher would sound more like, "Tell me about this part when you used [this], see anything there?" Or, "Here when you said [this], do you see how this connects to [this] over here? What is [this] telling you?" Engaging students in these types of conversations helps focus on learning instead of points. When students answer these kinds of questions, they will follow your lead and answer with nonevaluative comments about themselves, such as, "Well I thought [this] was how you did [this], I took [this] and put [that] here, but I see I needed to change [that] part too."

Practitioners largely underuse these types of dialogues because they are difficult for students to perform; when not performed properly, they leave participants feeling like the interaction did not yield any learning. Due to the nature of these exchanges, teachers often pass them over for more reliable techniques such as massed practice experiences, direct instruction, and individual reflection. However, done correctly and with fidelity, this step of reflective conversation and interaction has the most potential of all the steps to create the proper perspective of self and learning. This is how students should engage in these conversations, but what about the teacher's role?

To help this conversation process, teachers can inject themselves into the learning through reflective stances. This is very different than how a teacher may usually conduct a lesson, which is for pragmatic reasons related to activity logistics and content exposure. It is through these reflective stances that teachers must promote active inquiry and demand reciprocal discussion from students.

Linda Flower (1981), an expert in this area, states that students must "make meaning. First . . . make sense out of complex situations, and do so in words" (p. 4). This is the skill students must develop—the ability to articulate not only their current state of learning but also recognize and ask questions that are beginning to emerge from step 1 work. Flower (1981) goes on to state that a student "must use language to make meaning: that is, to name key issues, to describe their interrelationships, and to turn the sense of the whole into concepts expressed in words" (p. 4).

Fortunately, a teacher can use many strategies to promote student dialogue. One strategy could be to have students articulate why a certain approach did or did not work and what they learned and then compare their findings to the findings of their peers and the teacher or an expert. Following are some examples of questions teachers can use to prompt students to make these comparisons.

- ▸ What was your approach to this question?

- ▸ Did you get the same answer as your classmate? If not, why did you differ? What was your classmate's approach to the question? What can you learn from him or her?

- ▸ What did your teacher say was the best approach to the problem? Do you agree? What was similar or different about your approaches?

Another way to build these reflective dialogue skills is by having students process information through another student's point of view. This means having students act temporarily against their own views to challenge their mental framework, as outlined in the following questions.

- ▸ What was your teacher's approach to the question? Why did he or she use that strategy?

- ▸ Did you have the same answer as your classmate? Why did he or she use that strategy? If you had different answers, what might you learn from him or her to help solve this problem?

Lastly, teachers can have students search for alternative perspectives once they feel they have an answer. This temporary and intentional hesitation to lock in an answer can have a profound effect on learning. Consider the following questions.

- ▸ After listening to the class discussion, do you want to change your answer? Add to it?

- ▸ An expert in the field says that [new fact or information]. Now, would you change your answer?

These conversations not only produce stronger learners, but through this public justification, students can also develop social-emotional learning skills that include social awareness, relationship skills, empathy, and strategies for effectively reacting to errors and critical feedback. Ultimately, all this helps students develop learning resiliency by pressure-testing perspectives, breaking through delusions, and minimizing overconfidence. Following are some examples of questions that help promote this type of action.

- ▸ What did your classmate teach you about answering this question or these types of questions?

- ▸ What action steps did your classmate suggest that can help you raise your level of proficiency?

If we apply Flower's (1981) work to Buehl's (2011) taxonomy, we get the sample questions for step 2 that are organized into the chart in table 4.2. While this is similar to Bloom's taxonomy for learning, Buehl (2011) applies this same taxonomy to self-inquiry.

Table 4.2: Pair or Small-Group Conversation Guide (Step 2)

Level of Thinking	Comprehension Processes	Public Inquiry and Conversation Questions
Creating	Synthesizing Creating mental imagery	What does my work make you think about? What insight about your own work do you have after seeing mine?
Evaluating	Inferring	What are the most valuable parts of my work in your opinion?
Analyzing	Making connections Determining importance	What in your work has the most impact for me? How do you think I approached the problem? How did you approach the problem?
Applying	Making connections Inferring	What is the same or different in both of our work?
Understanding	Determining importance Inferring Creating mental models	Is this what you are trying to say in your work? Is this what you mean?
Remembering	Determining importance Creating mental models	What are three takeaways from your work? What are three things I can add to my work after seeing yours?

By using these types of questions, students can develop the skills needed to participate in a world of complex communication with others; when successful, these skills can help shape a healthy perspective of their current state of learning.

It is essential to remember that in the middle part of the lesson, as all students are fully aware of their current state of competency, we all use that awareness to grow each other to the expected competency of the lesson. The cooperative relationships that a teacher builds in his or her classroom can give rise to a strong sense of self for each and every student. It is important for teachers to have a wide array of cooperative learning structures and reflective activities to support this development.

And with the help of others, students can now contextualize the gaps in their learning properly and understand the relative value of their current state of competency. It is this shared environment that leads to the ability to self-regulate and manage one's own learning.

It is imperative that the engagement grows from a real-time reaction to student evidence instead of a preplanned cycling of different activities. The authentic engagement with material leads to a deeper connection to feedback and learning.

Past lesson plans require detailed steps about how a teacher takes students to and through learning. Our approach is the exact opposite, as it asks the teacher to outline detailed steps for how *students* will take themselves to and through learning. This means the teacher must plan for it and allow a self-regulatory learning environment where students are consistently describing their current state of competency. By asking students to advocate or defend their learning, you help students develop the skills of self-awareness and self-monitoring.

Concretize the Learning (Whole Group or Teacher)

It is not enough to simply show an exemplar during this whole-class segment of the lesson; in proficiency-based instruction, the teacher must not only model how to perform the skill or content application but also model how he or she thinks through it by using a think aloud. When the teacher models the desired state of mastery in both product and thought, students can compare their products and cognitive frameworks. It is this comparison of both cognition and product that creates proficiency.

Students must first recognize and articulate their states of competency, which they do in the first two steps. Next, in this step, students must come face to face with the reality of those competencies as they see them in relation to other students' competencies. Furthermore, they must understand how their competencies can potentially allow them to meet the expectations set forth by the course. Seeing the way to fulfilling these expectations is the foundation for efficacious learning, which ultimately is the sole purpose of school. This step must allow for the collaborative engagement of students and the shared responsibility of growing them toward the learning expectations. The activities in this step must allow for high interpersonal engagement, self-regulatory learning, and intense reflection on competencies.

Once the teacher builds a solid foundation in steps 1 and 2, he or she can then move on to step 3, in which the goal is to create a learning environment where all students work collaboratively with a shared responsibility for learning. In this step, the teacher promotes the idea of *interdependence*, which is predicated on autonomous, efficacious individuals and promotes quality feedback cycles between both teachers and students and their peers. This step creates a safe environment where making mistakes and making sense from those mistakes is the norm.

Proficiency-based teachers create a classroom environment in which students work interdependently with other students, as well as their teacher, to further develop proficiency. They understand that students, when demonstrating knowledge or performing a skill, rely on an interconnected framework of synthesized thinking patterns. These connected patterns, or mental maps (Schoemaker, 2011), may be faulty, underdeveloped, or even incomplete. It is the teacher's role to add context and details for the desired level of proficiency. In other words, the teacher explains to students the most logical and efficient manner they can move to the next level of the proficiency scale.

All students should enter this step with a clear awareness of their current state of learning, and it is the teacher's role to ensure that this current state aligns with what he or she expects within the proficiency-based target. In the example from figure 4.4 (page 60), a teacher would make sure students know they are able to read a geographical map with different measurement scales.

If a student feels that he or she can do the map reading with different scales, it is the teacher's role to add nuance to and contextualize level 3 (the level of proficiency) of this target to ensure that the student's mental map is durable. There are many ways to expose and scrutinize these mental maps. Following are some example questions to ask students.

▸ "How certain are you that your answers are correct? Did you guess? Are you unsure or sure they are correct?"

  ▸ **Example:** "When you were sure of your answer, did the strategy you used to solve the problem differ from my strategy? Why do you believe this to be the case? If you prefer your strategy to my strategy or your classmate's strategy, explain why (defend it)."

▸ "Which strategy do you think has the highest potential to produce the right answer?"

  ▸ **Example:** "Now that the activity is complete, what strategy will you use in the future?"

The outcome of step 3 is to develop a student's ability to use the surrounding community to gain an accurate sense of his or her proficiency. In other words, do they understand the realities of their proficiency? How does their new proficiency fit into the larger context of their community or life situation? During this step, teachers should promote the following skills.

▸ Viewing positives in others' work

▸ Adapting thinking to alternate points of view

▸ Using details about others' work to create new ways of thinking

If we apply Buehl's (2011) taxonomy one more time to our framework, we can determine questions to help students work within this step (see table 4.3).

Table 4.3: Proficiency-Based Whole-Class Reflective Questions (Step 3)

Level of Thinking	Comprehension Processes	Public Interdependent and Collaborative Questions
Creating	Synthesizing Creating mental imagery	How has your teacher or classmate changed what you understand?
Evaluating	Inferring	Which perspective is the most accurate? Mine? My classmate's? My teacher's? External?
Analyzing	Making connections Determining importance	Does the evidence confirm or disprove what you already knew? What is one part of your work that you would change now?
Applying	Making connections Inferring	How can I take what my classmate or teacher has said and add or change it to my work?
Understanding	Determining importance Inferring Creating mental models	What does my teacher want me to understand? What is my classmate trying to say? What is the impact of what was just said?
Remembering	Determining importance Creating mental models	What do I need to add to my work that will enhance its quality and grow my proficiency?

In this lesson-design structure, we aim to create an ability to relate one's own learning experience to a desired experience. A central outcome of this lesson design is the complete and proper articulation, or rather critique, of one's own work. The skill of being aware of one's own state of competence is the true expression of expertise, not the pursuit of a correct outcome (Wormeli, 2014).

Ultimately, what these three steps promote is student efficacy. When we create efficacy in learning, it affects the way we grade and report student performance and growth. We see grading as a fluid process based on emerging evidence of proficiency, and we see learning as a co-constructive process in which feedback is the grade.

Within this lesson-design structure, it is important that educators promote two key moments or realizations for students: (1) dissonance and (2) self-appraisal of evidence of competency. Both elements are required for students to fully realize and recognize their own competencies.

Dissonance

In the middle of the instructional diamond, it is important for the teacher to intentionally create moments of dissonance. Dissonance leads to students' ability to articulate, defend, and ultimately believe in their competencies. Teachers can create these dissonant moments by simply resisting the urge to inject themselves in evaluative ways into the learning. In other words, let students battle it out. By not engaging with students through evaluative lenses, teachers allow them to explore their beliefs about and confidence in their learning. This confidence is directly correlated to longer-lasting learning and overall satisfaction (Bandura, 1997).

Self-Appraisal of Evidence of Competency

Evidence of competency should not be simply "the stuff I know or am able to do." Instead we should also include "my perspective of the stuff I know and am able to do." An honest and accurate self-appraisal tends to be more in line with one's true competence than a third party's observation and evaluation of one's competency (Bandura, 1997). While students should assess their work at each part of the instructional diamond, in the middle of the diamond, they should collaborate and share responsibility to grow each other in the competencies outlined by the course.

While lessons should begin with individual student experiences, students should make sense of those experiences through reflective interaction with others. Therefore, the proficiency-based teacher uses the middle of the instructional diamond as a collective and shared moment for students to *realize* their competency levels and the potential for growth and development of those competencies.

Elaborate the Learning (Pairs or Small Groups or Individual)

As stated previously, continuous reperformance and analysis is essential for student learning and development. When students revisit their initial performance with a critical eye and an openness to feedback, they can experience significant insights and elaborations. It is essential that teachers practice this in their lessons and plan for it in their lesson design. We call this elaboration segment of the lesson *closing the diamond*.

Many teachers do a great job of engaging students in developing knowledge and skills, transitioning flawlessly from an initial performance moment to full class engagement. However, some teachers fail to bring the learning back to students to analyze, scrutinize, and elaborate on.

Teachers can *close the diamond* by initiating events that ask students to individually perform, contemplate, or observe the original proficiency experience again. These activities are similar to steps for *personalize the learning* or *scrutinize the learning*.

Insight 2: Lessons Should Close by Building Efficacy and Self-Reliance

We often hear teachers discuss with pride the exit slips that they develop for their classes. Unfortunately, in most cases, the assumption behind exit slips and the close of class is if some is good, more is better. We do not believe that after having completed thirty to forty minutes of mathematics, science, English, or social studies instruction that it is necessarily a good thing to do more of it. When we close lessons in proficiency-based instruction, we must build self-reliant learners. We build self-reliance by asking students to review the evidence they produced during the class for patterns of mastery. We must reserve the end of the lesson for students to review their own evidence and compare it to the proficiency-based target. There are several ways to close lessons in proficiency-based classrooms, including using reflective conversations and connecting current competency to future proficiency.

Use Reflective Conversations

Reflection and reflective conversations are key to proficiency-based learning. In proficiency-based instruction, students must consistently depend on their current state of learning as a foundation from which to grow and learn. It takes time to learn how to engage in these reflective conversations.

When we talk with teachers attempting to implement proficiency-based instruction, we often hear the following.

- **Students don't know how to self-assess:** Assessment and self-assessment are reflective interactions with an expectation. Students do not possess this knowledge and must be directly taught.

- **Students don't have the stamina to self-regulate learning:** Even if students *do* know how to reflect and effectively talk to their peers, they still don't have the stamina to do so. Most students don't want to do the reflective work. This is because points and letter grades have led students to believe that learning doesn't actually take stamina but rather quick bursts of energy. Think of these phrases students use about their schoolwork: *cramming and slamming* or *renting learning* (Guo, 2015). Students might say, "I will study for this test and get my grade up," instead of constructing learning in a balanced way over time by creating new, healthy mental models of how all the content fits together. Generally speaking, a mental model or construct is a cognitive representation of a perceived reality (Brown et al., 2014), and the health of these mental models is critical to learning.

- **Students don't have efficacy:** Students struggle to remain confident in their abilities to achieve the goals they have set for themselves.

Your goal as their teacher should be to instill the efficacy students need to feel successful and satisfied as they achieve their goals.

Even if students have the skills to self-assess, they might struggle to have effective reflective conversations with their peers. How many times have you heard students speak about their peers' work in a shallow way because they didn't take the time to look at the work, were trying to protect a friend's ego, or maybe didn't want to hurt a friend's feelings?

Danielson (2014) states, "A variety of forms and feedback, from both teacher and peers, is accurate and specific and advances learning" (p. 75). If students don't know how to have conversations about a third party's expectation (learning target), they may default to statements such as, "I just don't get what he wants, it's a ridiculous task anyway." On the other hand, students who have clarity of the teacher's expectation (learning target) may use the language of the target as a guide to have conversations that guide learning.

One teacher we observed asked us to watch what students were saying to each other during the lesson. Since the teacher was not using the target as an instructional tool, students simply talked about the memorized steps of solving the problem and attempted to mimic what the teacher taught them. Never did they discuss how they *perceived* their own expertise, nor did they ask their peers where they needed to take their thinking in order to solve it. We advised this teacher to have students reflect on their understanding and competency in relation to the learning target.

Connect Current Competency to Future Proficiency

Another way to build efficacy is to have students reflectively connect their current competency to future competencies and development since learning growth and development are fluid. The act of connecting your current state of competency to future goals and development is an important, efficacious action. Students will speak in a more self-prescriptive voice—for example, "The way I am using this vocabulary will lead to a clear message for my audience."

A teacher can get students to self-monitor in this way by avoiding diagnostic conversations with the student and, instead, forecasting conversations in which he or she asks the student to project current work onto a future event. For example, a teacher might ask, "So if you continued that vocabulary use, what might happen when you give your argument on Thursday?" The teacher sets up the student to assess his or her confidence and state of proficiency, essentially evaluating its validity.

Too many lessons end with simple emotional questions like, "Did you enjoy the lesson, and do you feel confident about the things you learned today?" Or, they might end with a small closing activity based primarily on discrete content for criteria. The beginning and the end of lessons should always reflect the expected mastery experience and the ability to grow and develop perceived efficacy.

When students begin to show autonomy in learning, the lessons become far less cookie cutter and more individualized for each student. This doesn't happen because the teacher individualizes the lessons but because students start to see knowledge through their own lenses. However, it is up to the teacher to begin evaluating any changes made from these insights for validity and impact.

Key Takeaways From Chapter 4

Review these key points with your team to reinforce the concepts from this chapter.

1. Proficiency-based instruction begins and ends with student performance. By building lessons that ask student to demonstrate their learning, teachers and students have visible evidence of their skill development, which informs the differing learning needs of each student.

2. Teachers should close lessons by building efficacy and self-reliance. We need to continuously hold students accountable for their own learning. This means that students need to develop the skill of self-assessment—the ability to express how well they know, understand, and can *do*.

Stop, Think, Reflect

With your team, reflect on the following two questions to continue with the collaborative process for change.

1. Collaborate to create formative assessments that can effectively and efficiently begin and end a lesson. In what ways do those assessments provide your team with evidence of student learning that can support stronger discussions about teaching and learning?

2. Compare and contrast the differing ways students reflect on their own growth as learners. How can you nurture skills of self-reflection so you can hold students more accountable for guiding their own learning goals?

chapter 5

Evaluation

Paying attention to how we evaluate change is an important consideration in any change process. This chapter focuses on how teams can analyze their change efforts. In proficiency-based instruction, assessing students is one half of the puzzle; the other half of the puzzle requires that teachers and teams make ongoing, immediate instructional shifts to help support learning as it is happening. How do they do that? Prior to implementing any change, teams must have an evaluation tool in place and ready to use. As educators, we need to react more immediately to our students' learning needs. This chapter highlights how to follow through on that commitment.

Following are four key points to remember during the evaluation stage.

1. Proficiency-based instruction is highly attentive to evaluation, continuously examining and responding to the learning needs of every student.

2. During the evaluation stage, teams commit to collaborating with one another around how they are making use of instructional strategies that facilitate learning more effectively and efficiently.

3. Teams must be mindful as they examine how well instruction improves learning. Team conversations should focus on instructional changes and action steps that lead to classroom learning.

4. Openly evaluating and scrutinizing proficiency-based instruction is a dedication to continuously examining the evidence of student learning and determining the value of instructional practices.

High-functioning teams continuously evaluate and reflect on the impact of their instructional practices. These teams recognize the relationship between teaching and learning, and their members ask themselves the question, "When I taught it, did students learn it?" By reviewing the evidence of student work, they take this question seriously by evaluating how well their lessons impacted the learning of every student. They examine whether students are demonstrating proficiency and how better instructional practices work to develop proficient learning.

Continuous evaluation is essential to our work with students because it promotes continuous improvement. We must evaluate the work we are doing and have ways of knowing how and why a change is or is not working. Ask your team, "What will indicate that we know we are doing better with our efforts to work in a proficiency-based instructional model? Does our proficiency-based instructional model deliver maximum impact on students' proficiency development?"

The following team story illustrates the evaluation process at work during its efforts to implement proficiency-based instructional practices. At this point in our team's journey, team members have prepared themselves with guided professional development around approaching curriculum, instruction, and assessment differently. They've brainstormed, thought together, had their doubts, explored each other's viewpoints, considered setbacks, and rehashed. Thus, they have worked through the process of change, and now they've decided to move forward with their shared and agreed-on insights. As a collaborative team, members have come to decisions they believe will help student learning and facilitate continuous growth.

At this point, notice how the team approaches how it evaluates its lessons. In what ways is it working toward continuous understanding and growth? How does its conversation reflect an open, honest, evaluative dialogue about making instructional improvements?

As you read the team's story, consider the following three challenges it faces during the evaluation stage.

1. As a team, teachers must challenge themselves to evaluate not only the learning data but also the effectiveness of their instruction.

2. Do the team's conversations focus on the effect of instructional practices on learning, or do team members avoid discussions about how to change instructional practices?

3. During the evaluation stage, teacher leaders must challenge teams to look closely at gaps in learning and help teachers encourage students to recognize those gaps in their own learning. In what ways are students the focus? In what ways are students' reflection abilities a concern for the team?

Our Team's Story

The team members spent the last few months focused on rebuilding their lessons to follow a more proficiency-based approach. With each new insight, they were determined to collaborate with their teammates in order to help all their students succeed. They were excited about discussing these insights, but more important for the team was to ensure their efforts were translating into real results for students.

One team norm that they wanted to focus on this year was to bring in evidence of student learning that demonstrated change. They wanted to hold themselves accountable to their mission: success for every student. They all knew this meant evaluating results, and they understood that sometimes their efforts only reached some of the students. Their goal for shifting to a proficiency-based instructional model was to reach every student.

At the next meeting, Marcos was excited to share his newfound observations on the benefit of the *you do first* model, and he got the sense that the others were just as excited to share their positive feedback about the shift they were trying to make. Marcos began the meeting with his positive observations: "I think the shift to students working with our skill expectations first was a really positive experience in my classroom. For one, it really helped me see their before and after evidence of learning. I brought in a few examples of their work to show you."

The team began to review the work samples Marcos brought in, and Sofie said, "Marcos, I think these are really interesting examples. I like that you brought in samples from a range of students. It looks like one student is struggling a bit with the writing strategies we are teaching, while another is improving and another is really doing a stronger job and looking to fine-tune her skills beyond our expectations."

Lauren added, "I see what Sofie is noticing, too. I have similar sample evidence from classes as well. It looks like a number of our students seem to be repeating similar struggles, and some are demonstrating that we could push them to greater levels of learning."

"I like what I'm hearing right now," Nico said. "In the past, we didn't have discussions like these until we were looking at our summative assessments. I'm interested in gaining more insights into our students' learning in the present tense so I can revise my instruction to help them reach success before summative assessments. As we look at their work now and evaluate our instruction, I think we might want to think about the kinds of interventions we should be including to help our students."

Tony looked at Nico and said, "I know what you mean, Nico. Last year, we were looking back on instructional problems and wishing we did our lessons differently. This year, we are looking at our students' work more immediately and changing our instructional practices so we are helping students to achieve right now. I want to show you the differences between my gradebook last year and this year. At this point in the unit, I'm able to tell you more about how my students are doing, what they are doing, and what I need them to do in order to be successful. And look, I'm seeing that many more of my students are moving toward our proficiency expectations this year than last year. I hope everyone is seeing improvements like this. I don't want anyone to say to me, 'You just have better students this year.' I want to make sure the changes I'm seeing in student learning have to do with the changes we are making in working differently and more effectively with each student."

As the conversation continued, there seemed to be a pattern in each team member's observations and reflections on his or her efforts to revise instructional practices. Patterns included better student engagement, more attentive conversations about learning, more student ownership, and what seemed to be an increased investment in the reflective activities of the class that they had once seen as nonessential activities.

Sofie said, "I really think starting with student work allowed me to be more authentic in the way I pivoted and directed the lesson. I noticed that my instruction needed to be more flexible as I was working with differing learning needs, and I noticed that my feedback to students was based more on the evidence of what I saw the students needing. I think proficiency-based instructional practices force me to really look at the evidence of students' work, and I know the changes are making them more intentional about the work they are doing in class. I find myself saying, 'Well, first you show me how and why you think you're developing the skills we are covering.' I ask them to point out and explain evidence of their skill development. In the past, students would make me read their work and identify if they were meeting expectations. I think the conversation has changed between me and my students."

Marcos said, "I know what you mean, and hasn't it made you approach teaching differently? Now we realize how important it is to pay attention and adjust to each student. I feel like the energy I put into teaching is more about my students and what is happening in my classes this year. I also think my students are learning to ask much better questions about what they are learning."

"I think they are asking better questions, too," Lauren explained. "More to the point, they are better able to state how they are meeting expectations or how and why they need to make improvements. Do you remember when students used to wonder about why they got certain grades? Now, my students are able to explain how they are working to develop their skills, and they are asking for advice and guidance about developing improvements to their learning."

Nico smiled and said, "I know what you mean. In the proficiency-based instructional model, the lesson is more focused on building a conversation about teaching and learning; it's not about telling and modeling and hoping students learn. I'm trying to teach my students to recognize that learning is a series of ongoing challenges. As I'm looking at their work and the way they reflect on their work, students need to be able to see learning as continuous improvement."

Tony added, "What I'm seeing in my students is similar. I think they are doing better at understanding the importance of their mistakes and are less afraid to take risks. When I look at their learning reflections and self-evaluations, I think they are getting better at explaining their strengths and areas for growth. This allows me to provide each of them with better feedback, too. Is anyone else noticing students reading feedback more seriously? In the past, they just looked at their grades and points."

"That's very true," said Lauren, nodding her head in agreement. "When I'm working in the diamond structure, I ask students to review feedback and read it. From there, we then set goals to use that feedback to inform improvements in learning. I think that is a valuable component to the proficiency-based instructional model, and it helps us evaluate progress in a much more authentic way. When students build goals off the feedback I'm giving them, I can develop stronger strategies that help them in more specific ways. I can also work with them in collaborative groups more effectively. The other day, I grouped them by their goals for learning, and that helped to create better peer-to-peer collaboration during the lesson."

"That's a really interesting way to work with the grouping component of the instructional diamond. So, did the students self-group?" Nico asked.

"Yes," Lauren responded. "They determined their own learning goals, and then I grouped them by similarities, which allowed me to work with them more directly. As we worked through the instructional diamond, students then presented their learning growth to the class, which was a really interesting way for peers to teach peers and for students to better understand the variety of different learning goals in our classroom. The diamond lesson seemed to create momentum of learning. Students needed to discuss their developing competencies more specifically, and they needed to focus on continuous improvement."

Marcos said, "For me, the successes of our changes have a lot to do with how quickly students are progressing. It sounds like everyone is working to help students progress in both self-directed and teacher-directed ways. More importantly, it sounds like students are seeing their learning grow over the course of our lessons."

"Yes, as I'm seeing it, I think we are helping students reach expectations in more attainable ways," Nico explained. "They are learning how skills develop and mature, and they are holding themselves and one another accountable to demonstrate skills in more visible ways. We should focus on how students are comparing their growth since the beginning of the year. In one of my lessons, I gave them past samples of each other's writing. That activity helped to reinforce new learning and establish further goal setting."

Lauren chimed in, "I like the diamond structure as well for many of the same reasons. The diamond structure helps us create our class lessons so they focus on how every student is developing competency."

Sofie added, "When we teach, we are always extending the development of a competency. I am reading a book by Albert Bandura (1997) about efficacy and competency, and he states how competency can be developed: perform it or directly practice it, observe someone doing it, visualize it, or develop it collaboratively within a group. That's how the kids in our classes should experience and develop competency."

Marcos said, "Let's make a graphic out of this idea and see what we get."

Sofie walked to the board and drew the following graphic of a proficiency-based lesson plan (see figure 5.1).

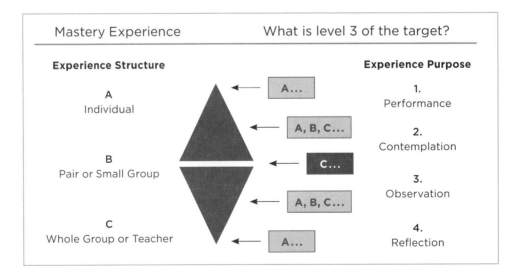

Figure 5.1: Proficiency-based lesson plan.

As she finished, team members observed that this was an interesting way to combine both the structure of the diamond and how to be more deliberate within each part of the diamond structure.

"I like this," Tony said. "I think it asks us to combine our observations of students with how we assess their learning growth."

Marcos added, "I think this is a pretty effective way of looking at lesson planning, and I already have some new ideas, as I never thought about the individual contemplation piece before. These four different approaches help me develop a variety of different entry points for each learner as well as better direct collaboration."

As the team began to close the meeting, Nico said, "Well, I think we are doing what we like to do most—improve on what we are already doing. I always like working with this team. Marcos, I think we are moving in a really good direction. I'd like to tinker some more with some of the things I heard today."

Marcos said, "I think we are all going to need to keep tinkering and reporting back to one another. But I think we are on a really good path toward making other positive changes as we head into the elaboration stage. At our next meeting, let's plan to discuss the changes we are continuing to make in order to effect positive changes for students who are still struggling or students who might need more challenges. I think we can start to tinker in ways that can really inform us how to build stronger interventions."

Four Competency Activities of Proficiency-Based Instruction

We support Bandura's (1997) concept of developing efficacy through competency. There should be an activity that promotes the intended competency and helps students develop it at each part of the instructional diamond, including performing, contemplating, observing, and reflecting. Note that these four activities can take place anywhere in the instructional diamond. It is not a progression per se, but a list of ways students can develop proficiency.

1. Students *perform* the intended competency, whether or not they have all the prerequisite knowledge or skills.

2. Students *contemplate* the intended competency, visualizing and articulating what they understand the competency to be and how they can demonstrate it.

3. Students *observe* others performing the intended competency in full.

4. Students *reflect* to consolidate, adjust, and build competency.

The developing competency of each student needs to be the focus of a lesson plan, which challenges all students to progress in their skills and abilities.

Activity 1: Students *Perform* the Intended Competency

In proficiency-based instruction, there are *expectations* and then there are *supporting content and skills*. Traditionally, educators have felt that in order to meet an expectation (proficiency-based learning target), students must first master *all* prerequisite skills or content before attempting the overarching mastery task. In proficiency-based instruction, we have found quite the opposite to be true.

We assert that with proficiency-based instruction, it is perfectly fine if students do not master, or even know, a supporting component before they begin working toward the proficiency expectation. Think about it . . . does a child know every part of a bicycle perfectly before he or she can ride it? No, the child begins riding and constructs the meaning of each bicycle part as he or she gains more experience while riding. Remember: the tip of the diamond is an initial experience of the expected competency, not the evaluation of competence.

With proficiency-based instruction, we expect students to demonstrate that they can retrieve (construct, deconstruct, and reconstruct) supporting pieces in different contexts. In fact, we suggest it is the reverse. Students present evidence of learning against the target (level 3) first and then deduce which of the supporting content or skills (level 4) led them to success or to realizing the need for improvement. To help you learn more about this concept, let's examine the difference between supporting content and expectations. Figure 5.2 shows the relationship between success criteria (the smallest, most granular curricular components) and the expectation (the proficiency curricular component of curricula).

Brown et al. (2014) support this idea: "Effortful recall of learning . . . requires that you 'reload' or reconstruct the components of the skill or material anew from long-term memory rather than mindlessly repeating them from short-term memory" (p. 82). In other words, students must learn the supporting skills and content to a learning target as they engage in activities related to it. To examine this point, we observed a science teacher during

Proficiency Scale: This scale will be used to communicate student progress in each learning target. This scale is also used to determine the final letter grade at the end of a trimester.

Exceeds 4	Meets 3	Approaching 2	Still Developing 1

Operations and Algebraic Thinking

Target: I can accurately solve problems using algebraic thinking.

4	I can accurately solve problems using algebraic thinking in a variety of contexts.
3	I can accurately solve problems using algebraic thinking.
2	I can accurately solve problems using algebraic thinking in a specific context.
1	I can accurately solve problems using algebraic thinking in a specific context with support.

Kindergarten Trimester 1 Criteria for Success

The following standards below are Trimester 1 criteria for meeting the targets. Please see the bold words for subject area and underline domains that correlate with the report card.

MATHEMATICS

Operations and Algebraic Thinking

Target: I can accurately solve problems using algebraic thinking.

- ☐ **K.OA.3** Decompose numbers less than or equal to 10 into pairs in more than one way, e.g., by using objects or drawings, and record each decomposition by a drawing or equation (e.g., 5 = 2 + 3 and 5 = 4 + 1).

Counting and Cardinality

Target: I can accurately identify age appropriate numbers in a variety of contexts.

- ☐ **K.CC.3** Write numbers from 0 to 20. Represent a number of objects with a written numeral 0-20.

ENGLISH LANGUAGE ARTS

Reading Literature

Target: I can effectively apply all applicable reading strategies to comprehend grade appropriate literature with prompting and support.

- ☐ **RL.K.1** With prompting and support, ask and answer questions about key details in a text.

- ☐ **RL.K.2** With prompting and support, retell familiar stories, including key details.

- ☐ **RL.K.10** Actively engage in group reading activities with purpose and understanding.

Reading Foundational Skills

Target: I can accurately and fluently apply grade-level foundational skills.

- ☐ **RF.5.3** Know and apply grade-level phonics and word analysis skills in decoding words.

- ☐ **RF.5.4** Read with sufficient accuracy and fluency to support comprehension.

Source for standards: National Governors Association Center for Best Practices & Council of Chief State School Officers, 2010a, 2010b.

Source: © 2016 by Antioch School District. Used with permission.

Figure 5.2: Learning targets and supporting skills and content.

a lesson prior to an exam. The target was to *effectively explain a scientific law in a variety of unstructured contexts.* During the lesson, the teacher told students that to achieve this target, they needed to understand five major content pieces. He proceeded to explain these five components in a visually distinct manner within several minutes. After this brief but complete explanation of the formulas, mathematics, vocabulary, and nuances of the target, the students practiced problems.

The students used the supporting pieces the teacher outlined as they attempted each problem. When a problem worked, they knew why; when a problem didn't work, they wondered why. They talked with each other about their work, and they attempted to clarify aspects of the problems with very specific questions. As they worked, they reflected and reflected some more.

When we asked the teacher about the lesson, he stated that it was just practice. However, in proficiency-based instruction, this is the ideal structure of a lesson. First, provide a simple outline of all supporting content that students need to reach the expected proficiency, and then outline the expectation, and go!

You might be thinking, "These students don't know the content yet. We need to teach it to them first." In response, we say, "Yes, we agree." However, we suggest that instead of teaching each supporting, prerequisite skill in a segmented, scaffolded, linear manner, we ask teachers to reveal the learning content students need to hit the target *all at once*, as they engage in proficiency-developing activities. You can achieve this by presenting all supporting content earlier in the unit or lesson.

Think about it like a cooking program on television. The chef usually states up front, "This is what we are going to make today . . ." and then proceeds to explain all the ingredients the viewer needs to make the dish. The chef doesn't teach one ingredient per episode, then another in the next episode, and so on. The chef presents all ingredients at the beginning and then makes the recipe, explaining as he or she goes.

This idea is the same for teaching in proficiency-based instruction. It sets the stage for what is called *active retrieval* (Brown et al., 2014). Active retrieval is the act of recalling content from long-term knowledge as opposed to recall from short-term memory. Students can retrieve knowledge if the teacher creates a consistent instructional process in which he or she asks students to *apply* supporting content or success criteria at different times and in different contexts related to the proficiency target (Brown et al., 2014).

For example, if the proficiency target is *I can consistently write arguments to support claims in an analysis of substantive topics or texts, using valid reasoning and relevant and sufficient evidence,* then the goal of instruction is to build this proficiency. A teacher can do this if he or she focuses instruction on writing argument activities in which students must apply the success criteria of focus, make a claim, reason with evidence, and demonstrate appropriate language and grammar in ways that show that they are making a proficient argument.

This is just like riding a bike. Parents montior and evaluate their child to ensure he or she can *ride a bike*. The child shows this proficiency by connecting and consolidating the success criteria of riding a bike, which includes using the handle bars and pedals, balancing weight, and so on. Teachers can apply this same instructional design in all content areas and grade levels because it is how students learn.

Why is this better than traditional lesson design and delivery? Without positioning supporting content and skills in this manner, teachers ask students to simply cycle learning through short-term memory or, as Brown et al. (2014) claim, to engage in "dipstick learning . . . [which] favors memorization at the expense of a larger grasp of context or creative ability" (p. 19). This kind of learning creates the illusion that students are proficient in a target when they have actually only grasped superficial aspects of the target.

Two key elements are integral when helping students perform an intended competency. First, teachers must engage students in the mastery experience. Second, they must follow up by creating an urgency among students to learn the material.

Engage Students in the Mastery Experience

At the onset of the instructional diamond, in each lesson, students must fully experience a version of the competency that teachers expect of them. We usually refer to an experience or event that a student uses and works through toward an expected competency as a mastery or competency experience. Generally, we reserve this experience for the penultimate event in a lesson or unit. It is more beneficial if students are fully immersed in a competency that is expected of them at the earliest moment possible in a learning cycle. Whether students fail in their first attempt is irrelevant; the more exposure to and experience they have with full competency, regardless of the outcome, the better.

Create an Urgency to Learn

In order to create an urgency to learn, the material must capture and develop the current state of students' proficiency. When students can see their current state of proficiency, it naturally creates an awareness of gaps that exist in and around that proficiency. This intuition is in each and every one of us as human beings; another person can't create this kind of urgency in us—we must create it ourselves. Students must therefore become aware of their needs and contextualize the gaps in their understanding and skill levels on their own. It is the teacher's job to create environments where this natural exposure occurs, so the natural urgency to learn can occur during students' formative development.

The primary way teachers can do this is by offering critical feedback with low consequence, such as by giving formative feedback during the assessment process. For example, during the writing process, the teacher provides immediate feedback to students about the organization or ideas for ultimate impact. In lessons designed to promote proficiency and continuous improvement, teachers should pre-think the kind of feedback students will need as they struggle or succeed in skill development.

Activity 2: Students *Contemplate* the Intended Competency

In the classroom, teachers should have as many nonevaluative and nonsummative interactions with a student as possible before actually evaluating that student. This fosters the ability to create co-constructed feedback and allows students the chance to learn how to grow themselves.

In proficiency-based instruction, students should perform, review, and reflect on each piece of evidence they produce. To be effective, teachers must resist the impulse to simply verify, or classify, students' work too quickly. They must allow students to "sit" with ungraded, unclassified assessment evidence while they think about it and study it as it relates to the proficiency-based learning target. We call this practice *pausing evaluation*.

To pause evaluation, the teacher gives students time to work with their evidence and simply inserts him- or herself into this process through reflective stances. Teachers using proficiency-based instruction must remember to extract evidence, challenge evidence, scrutinize evidence, and reshape evidence *before they rank the evidence*.

The idea of pausing is about teaching from reflective stances. Danielson (2007) states that teachers should "seize major opportunities to enhance learning, building on student interests or a spontaneous event" (p. 91). For this to happen, teachers must care less about what they think about a student's learning and more about what the student thinks about his or her own learning (Gobble et al., 2016). The goal of pausing evaluation is for teachers not only to verify the learning but to hold students responsible for verifying their own learning.

When helping students contemplate an intended proficiency, teachers must focus on exposing incorrect mental models and avoiding evaluative language, activities, or assessments.

Expose Incorrect Mental Models

One goal of proficiency-based instruction is to expose any incorrect mental models students have created and on which they base their learning. As previously noted, a mental model or construct is a cognitive representation of a perceived reality (Brown et al., 2014), and the health of these mental models is critical to learning.

These cognitive representations are the foundation of learning that a student relies on to grow. If any aspect of these models is faulty, learning and growth can become misguided, stagnant, or even negative, leaving students to possibly fall short of their potential. Thus, it is imperative that our instruction exposes these faulty models in order to truly help students grow.

Use Nonevaluative Language, Activities, or Assessments

It is tempting as a teacher to model the desired state of competency and help students produce their version of that desired state by reminding them of the essential components or understandings of that competency and allowing them time to view and recreate it. And along the way, during the lesson, the teacher simply checks in to verify that students are on the right track. In proficiency-based instruction, the teacher does not outline the desired state but instead, invites students to the desired state via nonevaluative language and interactions with the class. In other words, they don't reveal the desired state as a whole; they reveal it slowly to students by encouraging them to use their own thinking and reflection to discover it.

"What if I told you" questions are a great example of how teachers can do this. Using "what if I told you" questions in instruction creates instant reflection and self-evaluation as students re-examine their current state of proficiency with new bits of information. For example, "What if I told you that the author's message was about friendship and not teamwork?" The teacher uses the proficiency scale as a guide for students to work within a boundary for their reflection, so to speak.

For instance, if parents find their child's room messy and unkempt, they might be tempted to immediately tell the child that the room is not clean, stating, "This is where this toy should go" or "This is where the proper place for this item is," until the child has mindlessly obeyed and complied with the rules and regulations of a clean room. These parents would be better off simply inviting the child toward the desired state of the room through nonevaluative questioning and prompting, which ignites the self-motivation that is already inherent in the child. The parent would say in this instance, "Interesting place to put your clothes. What are some other places they can go?" or "What do you think the first thing someone would notice walking in here?"

The following are some of the advantages of using nonevaluative engagement with students.

▸ **Context or nuance:** By inviting and not ignoring context and nuance in learning and engagement, learning can become highly personalized and unique. Highly contextualized exchanges in learning can lead to more authentic buy-in from students as these exchanges stimulate the senses and expedite learning.

▸ **Interpretation or perspective:** By leaving exchanges open to interpretation and creating a safe place for sharing perspectives freely and openly, students can begin to share and, more importantly, hear their own thinking. This leads to the student trusting his or her abilities to express thoughts in effective ways. This not only builds trust in his or her own thoughts as a learning tool but builds the belief that his or her own thinking leads to growth.

▸ **Conceptions or misconceptions:** With nonevaluative stances students will begin to expose their faulty logic patterns and misconstrued learnings, which then enables them to process which patterns and learnings are correct and ultimately lead to success.

If, as teachers, we evaluate everything, then we may never expose misapplied or misunderstood learnings. It is these misconceptions that instruction must aim to expose and also reshape.

▸ **Variety of thought:** By using nonevaluative stances, we invite a wider variety of thought and action. Students must understand that their place of learning is a safe, exploratory environment where they can scrutinize their ideas openly and freely.

▸ **Quality feedback with relevance:** When a teacher approaches a student or addresses a class in a nonevaluative manner, this leads to students having to shoulder the burden of feedback. Teachers must use these stances consistently during instruction to ensure that feedback to the student is coming from the student. We can do this by asking questions such as the following (Barton, 1994).

> ▸ Why did . . . ?

> ▸ How would you explain . . . ?

‣ What other ways . . . ?

‣ How would you improve . . . ?

‣ Can you elaborate . . . ?

‣ Can you invent . . . ?

‣ Suppose you could . . . ?

‣ How would you change . . . ?

‣ What would you recommend . . . ?

‣ What would your friend say . . . ?

‣ Why is this better than . . . ?

‣ Would it be better if . . . ?

‣ How would you evaluate . . . ?

‣ What motivated you to do . . . ?

‣ What is _____ in your own words?

‣ **Feedback acceptance:** Nonevaluative stances and exchanges promote student thinking as the feedback. When the teacher provides feedback in a nonevaluative way, it means he or she teaches with what the student has articulated. This creates trust between teacher and student and makes the student feel the teacher is working more from kinship rather than autocracy (Gobble et al., 2017). This increases the chances that students will accept (trust and act on) feedback.

Being able to use nonevaluative stances through feedback promotes efficacy of thought in students and the belief that their thoughts are leading to growth and learning. This efficacy of thought should be a major goal of instruction.

Activity 3: Students *Observe* Others Performing the Intended Competency in Full

Teachers must remember that asking students to openly share and scrutinize their current competency, while it feels insecure and uncomfortable, has high value in learning. Also, observing the competencies of other students allows them to fully contextualize their abilities and the ways those abilities may or may not lead to the outcomes they desire.

The teacher must work hard to highlight the different understandings of each student and explain how each perspective can add to the group's understanding. This can be a moment of insecurity for both the teacher and students as they may never have had to face the reality of their competency, and the teacher may never have had to take such a critical and reality-based stance with his or her feedback.

One of the most effective ways to develop students' perceptions of proficiency is to engage students in class activities that allow them to compare and contrast their developing work. Teachers could implement this through gallery walks or peer-review activities that give students the opportunity to give each other ideas and feedback during the formative learning stages.

Activity 4: Students *Reflect* to Consolidate, Adjust, and Build Competency

It is not enough to have students simply state how the lesson went, identify strengths, or do more problems. Teachers must reserve the last part of the instructional diamond lesson for students to re-evaluate their proficiency and attempt to grow it, or at the very least review it in relation to future competency. This proficiency introspection leads to an increased awareness of their own growth and has a higher potential to build self-regulatory learning habits. It promotes the effortful retrieval of supporting content and skills, generative reflective structures, and time for elaborative thinking and thought development (Brown et al., 2014).

All these instructional practices support a type of learning that Brown et al. (2014) call *rule learning,* in which teachers ask students to become researchers of the underlying principles of material and use self-observation and self-regulation to determine what is desirable and if they are at the desired state.

Instead of a student studying the writing elements (such as tone, message, style, word choice) of one author's work and articulating what those might be, proficiency-based instruction asks students to look at several different authors' works, articulating the differences between them and ultimately reconstructing each author's elements (Brown et al., 2014).

Keep some of the following strategies in mind while students reflect on their learning.

Students as Archaeologists

Students must learn what it means to rely on their own thinking for their educational well-being, but teachers must be present to help them build this capacity. This is an important mindset to remember when implementing proficiency-based instruction, as this essentially changes the student's role in learning. A great way to think about this is as Danelle Elder (2012) suggests in her text *Standard Based Teaching: A Classroom Guide*: "Teachers must move from thinking of themselves as facilitators of a particular content to researchers of learning" (p. 15). Proficiency-based instruction is not for the teacher to find out where students are in their learning; rather, it is for *students* to find and understand where they are in their own learning.

Therefore, the role of a teacher in proficiency-based learning is to help students learn how to individually assess the state of their proficiency, articulate why they are not at the expected proficiency, and provide context and support to help them get there. Lesson design and delivery then must include reflective opportunities instead of directive ones. So how does this happen?

Brown et al. (2014) explain how to do this with the concept they call *dynamic testing*, determining the state of one's expertise. The authors state that the first step in dynamic testing is to determine one's own proficiency; then focus on areas of low performance; and finally, follow up with more testing to measure any improvement or the need to refocus.

In their practice of instruction and formative assessment, educators largely overlook the first part in Brown et al.'s (2014) process, determining one's proficiency. *We cannot state clearly enough that this part is the essential ingredient to proficiency-based systems and capturing students' states of learning.*

When we ask teachers to articulate the purpose of formative assessment, we typically hear them say that in order for students to truly understand where they are in their learning, they must not only understand teacher feedback but also apply it correctly. During formative assessment, students have a chance to get feedback on how they are acting on feedback. It is an essential cycle in the learning process. Determining one's expertise is the most essential part of instruction. Proficiency-based learning environments are predicated on students having an accurate perspective of their own learning as well as the skills to dig it out.

Proficiency-Based Reflection

Many teachers prompt students to reflect by asking, "How do you feel about what you learned today?" or "What did you learn today or still need to learn about the topic?" This is what we call *single-tier reflection*: students reflect only about the topic or material they learned. While single-tier reflection is beneficial, it still doesn't go far enough. Proficiency-based instruction relies on what we call *double-tier reflection*: students review their reflections, which is more commonly known as *metacognition*. Reflecting on performance is the first step. But reflection can't stop there. Students must take it a step further, analyzing the validity of their thinking. With double-tier reflection, students can move from thinking about their performance to knowing which thoughts can lead to better performance. Let's compare both single-tier and double-tier reflection:

Single-tier reflection is a holistic view of what occurred within one's work or performance and may only capture the emotional reactions. According to Ron Ritchhart, Mark Church, and Karin Morrison (2011), single-tier reflection takes two forms: (1) associative and (2) emotional. *Associative reflection* means that thoughts and data relate to student thinking but don't describe it. *Emotional reflection* means that a student's thoughts describe an emotive connection to the material and may not connect to next steps in his or her learning. In our observation, the majority of current student reflection is single tier; however, in proficiency-based classrooms, teachers cannot only rely on single-tier reflective structures. They need to deploy double-tier reflection as much as possible in order to help students reach proficiency.

Double-tier reflection is at an empirical level. It is about observing patterns of thought that students produce during the work. This means that students need to become intimate with the purpose of their thinking, something Ritchhart et al. (2011) call *meta responses*. Students produce meta responses by first recording an awareness of thinking and then validating that awareness. There are three components to performing double-tier reflection.

1. **Retrieval:** Simple recall of learned knowledge

2. **Elaboration:** Connecting new knowledge to what one already knows

3. **Generation:** Rephrasing ideas in new words of visualizations into new thinking (Brown et al., 2014)

While current reflective practices in education are mainly components 1 and 2, in double-tier reflection, we must focus on all three components. The idea of generative reflection is the most important of the three; without it, students will never do double-tier reflection.

The process of organizing thoughts into new combinations and structures is fundamental to effective reflection. This recombinant meta response builds the necessary learning stamina to handle a proficiency-based environment. Several ways to implement double-tier reflection follow.

▶ **Traditional reflection:** What is different from your work and the model?

Proficiency-based reflection: What is interesting about your work?

▶ **Traditional reflection:** What did you get wrong or right and why?

Proficiency-based reflection: What did you get wrong or right, and are you sure about the reason why?

▸ **Traditional reflection:** How did you arrive at the answer?

Proficiency-based reflection: Is the method you used to arrive at the answer the best way to go about it? Can you state other ways to go about getting the answer?

▸ **Traditional reflection:** Why is your answer correct?

Proficiency-based reflection: What can you do with the answer you have chosen?

▸ **Traditional reflection:** What is you work lacking (rubric indicators)?

Proficiency-based reflection: How is your own work making you think about your current state of learning . . . in other words, can you tell if you are at mastery yet?

Another way to promote evidence-based reflection is to provide guided activities that ask students to use double-tier reflection. In the example in figure 5.3, a teacher asks students to take their outcomes and scrutinize them against others in the class and even against the teacher's point of view. This is a relatively common practice; however, this teacher goes one step further and asks if students understand the thinking the teacher or classmate is using to arrive at the answer.

	Student Answer	Most Popular Answer Over Last Five Years	Teacher Answer (Suggested, Not Final)	Peer Answer
Question 1 (Selected Answer)	A	B	A	C
Tier 1 Reflection	Why did you answer that? Why is the correct answer the correct answer? What was your approach to the question?			
	Show Correct Answer: B			
Tier 2 Reflection	What did your partner teach you about answering this question correctly? What did your teacher suggest as the correct approach to answer this question? Did your approach differ from the teacher's? Defend your strategy if you think yours is more effective.			

Source: Adapted from Elbaum, 2015.

Figure 5.3: Sample double-tier reflection activity.

When students are able to discuss learning and self-assess how well they are demonstrating skills, they become more independent in their capacity to learn and continue learning without a teacher.

For so many years, educators have stressed a commitment to build lifelong learners. In this chapter, we explored key ways that teaching teams can build strategies into their lessons that focus on the capability of students to self-assess their developing abilities and learn to progress in their development.

Key Takeaways From Chapter 5

Review these key points with your team to reinforce the concepts from this chapter.

1. Teams should meet regularly to reflect on and evaluate their approach to a proficiency-based instructional model. What are the signals and the evidence that a commitment to proficiency-based instruction has an impact on student growth?

2. Teams need to pay close attention to their instructional capacity to develop every student. Remember, in every classroom, a teacher is working to develop *all* students. Be sure to evaluate how developing students respond differently to instructional strategies. What is working and not working? Likewise, evaluate what works for students who are functioning at high levels. Proficiency-based instruction helps teams reflect on how they are working to grow all students.

3. One key feature in this chapter focuses on building the abilities of students to self-assess their development. At certain points in a lesson, students should be able to self-report how they think they are progressing in their knowledge, understanding, or ability to demonstrate a skill.

4. Teams that come together to evaluate their efforts begin to compare and contrast ideas; seek alternative, innovative approaches to teaching and learning; and work to address needed changes immediately. As teams work to reconceive lesson planning, the evaluation stage allows them to recognize the positive changes they are making and refocus on differing ways to support students.

Stop, Think, Reflect

With your team, reflect on the following two questions to continue with the collaborative process for change.

1. The value of proficiency-based instruction is that it continuously monitors student growth. How is your team responding to evidence of student learning? Are all students getting the help they need to support their potential?

2. What are the challenges and demands of teaching lessons that are focused on developing student proficiency? In what ways is your team collaborating to support every teacher to implement proficiency-based instructional practices more effectively?

chapter 6

Elaboration

As teachers and teacher teams become stronger at developing proficiency-based instruction, they begin to elaborate on the good strategies and techniques that respond to every student's learning needs. This chapter discusses how proficiency-based instruction is focused on constant inventiveness. A shift to proficiency-based instruction requires a teacher to consider how instructional practices can be flexible and adaptive enough to help all students as they are developing. Later in chapter 7 (page 117), you will find tools and sample lesson plans to help you develop your own proficiency-based lesson plans.

At the evaluation stage, the team questions how well the new idea is working, notices patterns and trends in data, and identifies the degree to which the idea is a winner or loser. In this stage, the team is responsible to make necessary adjustments toward immediate improvement.

Following are three key points to remember during the elaboration stage.

1. Like each stage in the change process, the elaboration stage is about continuous improvement. In this stage, elaboration can be about fine-tuning or adding nuance to instructional changes.

2. During this stage, the team sees the value of proficiency-based instructional practices, and they want to build on it or revise their ideas. At this point in the journey, the team members are also ready to serve as teacher leaders, sharing their struggles and successes with other teacher teams that might be working to change, too.

3. At this point, the leader supports the value of continuous improvement and the values around success for every student. The leader might ask, "Is this change working for every student or just a subgroup of students? How so? If not, how might the change be more beneficial for more learners?"

As educators, the elaboration stage should feel natural as we work to add nuance to and revise our teaching. The only downside to this continuous growth mindset is that everyone walks around saying, "When is good just good enough? Can't we just leave it all alone this year?" Although this can sound like exhaustion or frustration, the point of our work is to push our instruction—and our schools and student learning—forward.

During the elaboration stage, the team recognizes the strengths of its collaborative insights, and its members build up ideas and tinker with them to develop learning more deeply. One point we want to stress: elaboration is the immediate response to evaluation. The elaboration stage is an ongoing and thriving process of collective inquiry. It springs forward from a results-driven decision-making model. Now that we've followed our team this far, we want to restate that the process of change is not linear or step by step. The elaboration stage is a rich example of that point. Individuals and teams will likely dip back into preparation. For instance, they might want to review previous learning or explore more sophisticated understandings. They might slow down and incubate ideas after evaluation. They will certainly develop insights during the elaboration stage. The team will notice that the process is recursive, and team members will begin to collaborate with momentum.

When reading about our team's journey, consider how the entire elaboration process should not be about struggling to understand but, instead, about turning good ideas into great ideas. Identify how the team starts to build up new and better ways to implement proficiency-based instructional practices and how it is seeing the immediate benefits for students.

As you read the team's story, pay attention to the following three challenges team members face during the elaboration stage.

1. The team members must embrace the idea of healthy dissonance in their instruction. The team begins to pay attention to the benefits of student dissonance and looks for ways to help students productively struggle forward in their learning.

2. The team begins to see the benefits of proficiency-based reflection and that students lack the reflective stamina necessary to grow their own learning. The team explores strategies and practices to build this stamina and ability in its students.

3. The team members challenge themselves and each other to think about more ways to promote efficacy and self-reliant learning. The team discusses how to incorporate this concept and belief into its assessment and instruction.

Our Team's Story

As they progressed, the team members became more and more aware of how changes in their instructional practices were affecting student learning. They were a results-driven team, and they spent their collaborative time reviewing student work and the evidence of student learning. They also saw areas for growth. Marcos framed the meeting by concentrating on what it means to elaborate on the ideas they were generating. He wanted to focus on some of the concerns the team was having, and he wanted to stress the importance of continuous improvement.

Marcos began the meeting by reviewing a number of the positives. "As we begin to dig deeper into our instructional practices and as we begin to really address some of our concerns," he began, "I think we want to spend some time summarizing our accomplishments in our efforts to shift our lesson planning to a proficiency-based model. We've hit upon three major changes: (1) revising the format of our lessons with attention to student proficiency; (2) shifting to a diamond-shaped instructional plan that helps develop competency during a lesson; and (3) focusing on how our students can reflect on their own learning development. Our focus this year has been on growth and how our instruction can better nurture growth on a daily basis and over time."

Sofie said, "I'm really proud of those three overhauls, and I've learned a lot about my own teaching and how I can work better with students. I also want to remember that every week we discussed concerns about our teaching practices, and I think we should continue to focus on how we can elaborate on our ideas so we are continuing to work for every student."

"That's right, Sofie," Nico said. "The most difficult aspect of our work is that it is always changing because our students are always changing. As I've been reviewing the year, I have noted one important area for us to pay attention to is the area of inconsistent growth in our students. I've heard all of us talk about certain students who seem to be moving in a good direction one week only to slip backward the next week."

"I know what you mean, Nico and Sofie," said Marcos, "and at this point in our work, I think it is really important for us to unpack some of the strong points and readdress the areas we've been concerned about. We've been approaching instruction very differently, and I think we want to review and revise our work based on our reflections."

Tony said, "I think we should focus on the instructional diamond and where we think we can elaborate on our ideas. Let's break down our discussion with the visual we refer to in our collaborative discussion of lesson planning." Tony posted the following graphic (see figure 6.1).

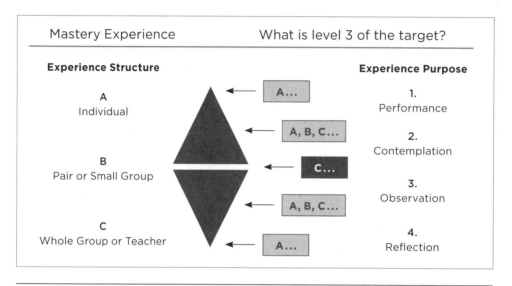

Figure 6.1: Instructional diamond lesson-plan template.

"When I refer back to this model," Tony continued, "I know that I need to pay close attention to how I'm building the early individual assessment during the first part of the diamond. As I'm looking back on the year, I think I need to concentrate on making sure those individual experiences allow students to really show what they know, and I'd like for us to work on crafting those experiences in more authentic ways. What I'm trying to say is that I think those initial experiences of each lesson should work to engage the students in a way that allows them to demonstrate skills vividly and self-identify gaps in their own learning."

Lauren said, "I think you are noticing what I'm noticing, too. I think we will want to really focus on elaborating our work so that our students are developing a stronger, more self-reflective ability to recognize what they know, understand, and can do and where they have areas of growth. I've noticed that my students sometimes lack the stamina to think reflectively. Some were very good about developing that skill, but many of my students still have a difficult time self-critiquing their own work. I notice that some of their peers struggle to provide the feedback that might be effective enough to impact one another's learning."

Marcos added, "I think those are two important areas for us to concentrate on during our lessons, too. It sounds like we might want to look at some of the strategies we use and how we might be able to rebuild some of those strategies so that they are more effective in the way students communicate. I remember Nico worked to build discussion guides that led students through different types of questions to help guide peer-review feedback. I used some of his ideas and added a few ideas to help guide my students during the first part of a lesson, and the strategy really helped focus my students and helped them to reflect."

Sofie said, "That's the kind of work I think we need to concentrate on. I remember that same guide Nico created, and my students responded really well. In some ways, as I look over the year a bit, I think we could focus on creating self-reflective and peer-to-peer tools that can help support learning on a level that can engage students in building self-confidence as well as self-critiquing skills."

Lauren built off Sofie's thought. "I like what you're saying," she said. "I think that suggestion refers back to some of our earlier discussions in which we talked about how students display inconsistencies in their developing abilities. I think we really want to concentrate on making sure that our instructional practices change in two ways. We want to make sure students are showing us that they are competent in their learning. We want evidence of learning. We also want students to leave our classrooms with a steady grasp of how they can address the gaps in their learning. For me, this means making sure we elaborate on our process of interventions. Let's face it, from our evidence, some students write reflections expressing that they still might be struggling to grasp a concept or a new skill."

"That's certain," agreed Nico. "By the end of a class period, I know a number of my students are still struggling. I'd like for us to focus on two steps in using the instructional diamond. First, we must determine what experiences occur at each part of the diamond—at the tips, middles, and center. The first decision is the experience *structure* (individual, pairs, or whole class), and second is the experience *purpose* (perform, contemplate, observe, or reflect). Second, I'd like for us to unpack creative ways to teach at each part of the diamond as we teach new concepts or extend learning. I think I have a lot of room for growth in that area, and I still fall back into some traditional practices when I teach. A few times this year, I tried some of Lauren's strategies that allowed students to work with me to teach ideas, and the learning experience was much more collaborative and student centered. I'd like to elaborate on ways to do that more effectively."

Marcos said, "I'm taking some really good notes about your ideas. I'm trying to keep a list. So, it sounds like we are focused on two points right now. One is on the student reflection piece, and the second one focuses on extending learning with supportive strategies and more immediate interventions."

Tony said, "Those are my biggest concerns."

Sofie added, "Yes. I think our conversations about the second part of our diamond graph have been successful, and I'm sure that side of the graph could use more attention, too. I think if we integrate the two sides of the graph—paying attention to them in a more integrated way—we could make some significant revisions that help us emphasize student learning and growth."

Lauren added, "Right. I think those learning experiences could provide more dissonance for the variety of learning that is going on in the room. At times, I think some of my students didn't feel dissonance in their learning. They thought parts of the year were easy. I'd like to make sure that all of our students walk out of the room challenged appropriately, almost as if the class is always a little difficult for everyone, every day—but not impossible."

"That's so true, Lauren," Nico agreed. "I think at times we need to do a better job with progressing students over the course of our units. Maybe if we looked at our lessons as interlocking more, we might be able to address that concern. I think we need to think more about how our lessons are soliciting evidence over the course of the unit, not like lessons that stand alone by themselves."

Tony said, "I actually plan for the moments when students will be struggling, and I'm not afraid to let them struggle a lot. I think the instructional diamond invites us to push students to develop their potential. But I agree, I need to get better at making sure I'm following up with students with interventions that help them achieve. I sometimes think that I'm pushing students and then off they go to another class, and that's when my job with them ends. But that is not the way I want to be as a teacher. I want them to learn. So, I think I could use help with interventions, too."

Sophie added, "Maybe our team conversations should focus on those two points: (1) What do we do if students haven't learned? and (2) What do we do when they have learned? I'd like us to collaborate more on those two questions."

Nico said: "Yes, I think that can help us grow student learning and also help students to grow their own learning. If we are working to help students become college and career ready, we need to focus on building their self-efficacy. I'd like our competency graph to include an expectation for confidence." Tony drew the graph they had considered earlier in the process (see figure 6.2).

Marcos said, "I believe that fostering this confidence in relation to competency development is the main goal of all education."

Nico paused and said, "I know I sound passionate, but this change to instructional practice has really opened my eyes to what the true purpose of school is."

"But how do we promote this in our classrooms?" Lauren asked.

Marcos said, "Well, I tried asking students prior to formative assessments how confident they were that they were going to get the right answer and explain why. During the exam, I asked some questions such as, 'At this point in the assessment, do you still feel confident that you will receive a proficiency mark?' and after the assess-

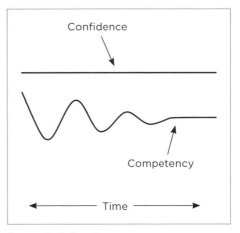

Source: Reibel, 2018a.

Figure 6.2: Efficacy as it relates to confidence in competency development.

ment, before I gave the answers, I asked the confidence question again. This repeated confidence check not only gives me the information I need as a teacher to help students more effectively, but it also creates a clearer reality of proficiency for the students." To highlight this, Marcos wrote the following on the board (Reibel, 2018a):

1. Learn how to create my own competency.

2. Verify the validity of my own competency.

3. Foster the belief in my ability to create, validate, and maintain my own competency. (p. 20)

After he was finished, Marcos explained, "It is the belief we have in our competencies that allow us to hit our goals, pursue our interests, succeed in the way we have defined it, and be satisfied with our lives."

To close the meeting, Marcos continued, "I'll summarize a quote I read in *The Assessor* magazine: We must remember that teaching is not simply about making a difference in a student's life, it is primarily about helping students make a difference in their own (Reibel, 2018a). As we continue our work in proficiency-based instruction, I think we should focus on that point. It can help us to guide the revisions we suggested today."

As the meeting ended, Marcos promised to send out a list of the collected revisions to work on, and the team spent some time setting up action steps to make immediate revisions to their lessons based on some of concerns they listed.

Seven Elaborative Practices of Proficiency-Based Instruction

At this stage of implementation, teachers begin to add to and expand their proficiency-based instructional practices. We typically see the following seven elaborative instructional practices at this stage in a teacher's learning.

1. See feedback as a conversation, not a comment.

2. Include summative evaluations earlier in the learning process.

3. Cultivate learning stamina.

4. Build learning confidence.

5. Create learning tension.

6. Personalize the learning.

7. Provide enrichment opportunities for students who have already mastered the content.

Practice 1: See Feedback as a Conversation, Not a Comment

In proficiency-based instruction, teachers think about feedback as more than just comments on the paper. Instead, they think about feedback as a session. When we think about a session, we think about people interacting deeply about information and concepts. When we think about comments, we simply think about one-sided conversations. Evidence-based reporting is based on conversational feedback sessions in which both parties become highly aware of each other's comments about emerging proficiencies.

During instruction, we cannot view feedback in isolation. Students must understand and feel its importance for their growth. Therefore, we should not view feedback simply as comments but more as sessions (Brookhart, 2017).

When we view feedback as comments, students tend to see them as "throw-aways," statements that they cannot do anything about. When we use feedback in the correct manner it becomes prescriptive and forward facing, increasing its value.

For example, instead of stating, "Your work on polynomials was not that great," the teacher can say, "The way you are graphing polynomials will lead to problems with graphing quadratics." This statement is more effective in many ways. First, it acknowledges the current state of the student, for example: "The way you are doing [that] is not going to lead to success." Notice that this doesn't state what the student is currently doing wrong. It simply implies that while the student might be growing his or her learning, it may not be in the most efficient way. It is suggestive, not declarative.

Second, this statement is future facing. The feedback statement is acknowledging the future state of the student's learning through the lens of his or her current competency.

Third, it suggests that nothing is set in stone. It suggests to the student that there is still time to reflect, time to learn, and time to adjust what he or she is currently doing.

Fourth, it is evaluative. Notice that neither the current state nor future state of this statement suggests that anything is classified. "The way you are doing [that] will lead to [this]" is neither evaluative nor punitive, and instead promotes growth and efficacy in a student's learning. Proficiency-based instruction must use feedback to connect current competencies to future competency. This means that the feedback must be a statement of what is but also connect to what could be . . . good or bad.

By providing feedback in this manner, we increase the likelihood that students will use the feedback, and the more they use it and feel it helping them, the more they trust it and ultimately trust the teacher. Students must explore, internalize, and act on feedback throughout instruction, and they won't do so unless they trust it. Trusting feedback almost certainly leads to growth.

Proficiency-based instruction asks that the students perform the intended competency early and often and retrieve the needed supporting content or skills while doing so. This allows them to connect and synthesize knowledge into layers of proficiency that can all be connected. By engaging in the intended competency throughout their learning, students can have more time to apply and create proficiency, which helps them apply the material for the long term and thus promotes lasting proficiency.

Practice 2: Include Summative Evaluations Earlier in the Learning Process

Evaluation, to most, suggests finality. It is because of this perspective that teachers generally view summative evaluations as an ending event that they use to verify learning. However, in proficiency-based instruction, the word *evaluation* doesn't necessarily mean the end of a learning time frame; in fact, it can even mean the beginning.

In proficiency-based instruction, summative evaluations can occur early. It is a key aspect of proficiency-based instruction because it sets the stage for all learning that takes place afterward. This practice lessens the high-stakes nature of the judgment experience, allows the students to see it as valuable feedback, and most importantly, creates time for students to learn and reflect.

Let's examine the bicycle analogy again. When a child starts riding a bicycle, he or she may fall on the first attempt. The child's parent or guardian then gives feedback and new information for the child to use as he or she attempts to ride the bicycle again.

What is happening in this scenario is the child has a summative evaluation experience early in the learning process, and now all future learning can relate to it, which can help contextualize and foster growth. This scenario highlights the reason why teachers must work the same way in proficiency-based instruction. Teachers must move up the evaluative experience in the pacing to allow students time to gain perspective from it and actually learn from it.

When a teacher places the evaluative experience earlier in a unit of study rather than at the end, students have a higher potential to fail early, but they also have time to react to the feedback, accept the status of their learning, and gain the opportunity to change the trajectory of their growth.

A common entrepreneurial mantra is "Fail cheap, fail quickly, fail often," and the same holds true with this notion of early summative evaluations. When allowed to fail earlier, students fail "cheaper," meaning the event has inherently lower stakes because there is now time to learn and recover. When teachers do not move up the evaluation, students have no time to reflect and react to the feedback from it.

Practice 3: Cultivate Learning Stamina

In the end, it is essential that teachers build students' learning "muscles" and stamina. Students simply do not have efficacy of reflection when they enter school, and, unfortunately, they haven't gained it by the time they exit the school system. With the inability to reflect appropriately, students struggle to understand how to articulate their learning and their emotions, potentially leaving them to become apathetic and despondent. Unfortunately, bad outcomes can occur because students simply don't have the cognitive or emotional stamina to make responsible decisions or engage respectfully (Bandura, 1997).

Proficiency-based instruction should be a continual process of assessing and reflecting, both formally and informally. This process can build a student's ability to focus, self-sustain, self-direct, and remediate problems, which are skills he or she will need to participate as a national and global citizen. Using proficiency-based instruction to build academic and emotional endurance can create a solid foundation from which a student can demonstrate proactive, prosocial behavior in the classroom.

Practice 4: Build Learning Confidence

As defined previously, students develop efficacy when they build their own proficiency and become more confident in making their learning happen. Figure 6.3 shows the profile of an efficacious student. In this representation, competency has not taken hold or even started to develop, yet this student is still confident that he or she can move from a non-competent state to a competent state.

While this correlation may be obvious, as educators, we typically do not plan or deliver learning in this manner. We must begin to embrace the reality that confidence in oneself is a necessary goal of all instruction and assessment and the more we allow students to experience the natural oscillations in their own learning, the more confident students will become in their learning (Reibel, 2018a).

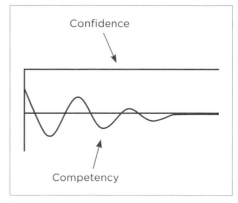

Source: Reibel, 2018a.

Figure 6.3: Confidence of an efficacious learner.

One way to do this is to ask students how confident they are in their proficiency before, during, and after any event. Table 6.1 shows some questions you can ask students to gauge their efficacy.

Table 6.1: Building Efficacy in Assessment

When	Key Question
Before Assessment	Am I confident my current state of proficiency will lead to success?
During Assessment	What am I realizing about my proficiency as I engage in the event?
After Assessment	Based on my realizations and results, am I confident in my future proficiency?

By asking students to constantly work with, be aware of, and analyze their proficiency, we can create a safe environment for failure and experimentation, which leads to an environment that fosters confidence and efficacy.

Asking questions that make students think is where we've all lived up until now as teachers. Socratic method, higher-order thinking questions, essential questions, and thematic questions are all tools we continue to use to generate thinking. The goal now is to generate confidence and the belief students have in their own competencies and help them see how those competencies lead to achievement and success of their goals. Simply being aware of their own thinking or answering difficult questions does not build this ability known as efficacy, but asking students to take a self-reliant approach to their learning can develop a stronger sense of self and a more confident, responsible learner. Simple questions such as "So now what can you do with that information?" or "What can we now do with that skill?" create self-referent learning in which students see themselves as the object of their own development. The connection between actual competence and students' perceived competence becomes a potent instructional tool for the teacher.

Practice 5: Create Learning Tension

In this stage of lesson development and instruction, it is important to allow dissonance to occur. Essentially, teachers should intentionally create tension points in the lesson and then pivot it in the direction the students want. For example, after leading students to a specific conclusion about a story's main character, an English teacher can add in an additional detail that invites students to reconsider their conclusion. When a learner is forced to reconsider their current state of learning based on new information or concepts, this creates a learning tension point. This is not easy to do, as tension points can cause stress and anxiety. Teachers create dissonance when students are at their learning threshold.

Furthermore, the awareness of when to change the lesson's direction and how is a skill that teachers must develop. These dissonant moments are ripe for an introspection that can provide students with personalized insights into their competency and can increase efficacy.

Proficiency-based instruction involves teachers reacting to student-produced evidence. This means that teachers must be equipped to not only generate evidence but more importantly, properly react to student-produced evidence. They must maintain reflective engagement to help students develop self-reliance.

No teacher knows exactly how long proficiency takes to develop in a student; therefore, we cannot structure our instruction into chunks of time. We must determine the time when learning tension is necessary to peak interest and highlight a learning purpose.

The timing and structure of learning tension depends on the skill component or content that is lacking. If it is a small component but has a big negative impact on one's proficiency, then it may be a quick comment that solicits insights. Or maybe it is a larger segment of learning that requires a more nuanced build up. For example, an English teacher might comment to her class, "Remember, thesis statements highlight your position in relation to a topic, not simply state the theme of your paper." Teachers must determine and create tension points when they are reacting to student performance or evidence, not when they are planning.

Practice 6: Personalize the Learning

In a proficiency-based classroom, student evidence is ripe with conceptions and misconceptions, thought patterns and irregularities, and so on. But some teachers still insist on bypassing all this to directly present material and assess whether students learned it. To properly capture current states of learning, teachers must use student-generated thinking, comments, and insight to drive a lesson. By doing this, teachers can make the lesson more personally relevant as students begin to see their personal thoughts, actions, and reactions as valuable to their growth and development.

As the lesson is dynamically unfolding, a teacher must be an *empirical examiner* of learning, collecting and directing student thoughts and work as it happens. The teacher can then move the lesson in an immediate and authentic direction based on the current state of each student. For example, as students engage in a dialogue about the Declaration of Independence, a teacher might notice that the students are only engaging shallowly with simple details and basic information. The teacher could then post details or information on the board and invite students to begin immediately using them in their dialogue.

This approach may be different for some teachers, as there is a general tendency in teaching to complete the activity and move on to another, and then another, until the assessment comes to see if students know the Declaration of Independence.

Note that the teacher doesn't wait to assess. The teacher's interactions with students during this instructional moment act as assessment, because he or she knows they are only using simple details and basic information. The teacher immediately corrects the trajectory of student learning by offering insights, information, or details that students should be using.

We see many teachers plan lessons that are beautifully polished and organized, like a debate or Socratic dialogue, where not even a single screw is loose in the chassis of the lesson. However, if you observe closely, the quality of student cognitive engagement and thinking may be actually quite shallow and superficial.

Danielson (2014) states that a proficiency-based teacher is "constantly 'taking the pulse' of the class . . . monitoring of student understanding is sophisticated and continuous" (p. 75). Many teachers misinterpret the word *sophisticated* to mean a highly complicated series of activities that increase in difficulty over time. What sophisticated means, at least in a proficiency-based classroom, is a teacher's expert ability to use student evidence in instruction. How else would you constantly be able to take the pulse of the class? There is no formative assessment product fast enough to do that.

Teaching dynamically with in-the-moment student evidence is a skill that is difficult to develop and even harder to have embraced with confidence. We hope you are beginning to understand the value of proficiency experiences, have embraced the instructional diamond to produce generative learning, and now consider all moments in your classroom as those to prepare students for proficiency, develop students' proficiency, or determine students' proficiency.

We have seen many teachers master this skill in a short time when they consider these mindsets and tools carefully and embrace the idea that all students have the ability to grow themselves if teachers just create the space for this to happen. It is essential to capture authentic current states of learning to personalize the learning. To a teacher trying to uncover current states of learning, providing opportunities for students to show their misconceptions, faulty patterns, logic, and recognition patterns is invaluable for developing lessons that are personally meaningful to each student.

Practice 7: Provide Enrichment Opportunities for Students Who Have Already Mastered the Content

As previously noted, there are four levels of proficiency: (1) foundational skills, (2) approaching expectations, (3) meeting expectations, and (4) excelling expectations. All these levels are important, as shown in figure 6.4.

Level 4: Excelling at Someone's Expectation
Level 3: Meeting Someone's Expectation
Level 2: Approaching Someone's Expectation
Level 1: Foundational Skill

Figure 6.4: Levels of proficiency.

In proficiency-based instruction, it is important to remember that learning doesn't have a ceiling. Even when we have mastered an area of our lives, we continue to extend that mastery into new skills, knowledge, hobbies, and connections. The same goes for instruction. Many say, "Who cares about level 4?" Or teachers might tell students that they can achieve the fourth level any way they see fit. With this perspective, we run the risk of instruction stalling out and disengagement in student learning.

However, level 4, or what we call enrichment or extension, is a very important part of the instructional process. Level 4 does the following.

▸ **Validates rigor:** Level 4 helps validate the rigor of the other three levels; teachers must calibrate their view of level 4 to verify that level 3 has the correct rigor.

▸ **Helps outline the idea of growth:** Simply by its existence, students see the importance of their new learning and where it is taking them.

▸ **Contextualizes level 3:** By discussing level 4, teachers can verify that level 3 is written correctly and is clear.

▸ **Keeps instruction moving:** A student at level 4 can continue his or her learning while others are still working and achieving proficiency.

▸ **Supports effective self-assessment and reflection:** Without level 4, students have no context for how they have learned, what they have learned, and what they can do with the new skills. The purpose of level 4 is not only for self-assessment but also for allowing students to see where their new learning and newfound insights can take them.

▸ **Validates whether a student is at level 3:** By offering level 4 activities and assessment questions, the teacher can gather evidence to validate whether the proficiency is really there.

The purpose of the elaboration stage is to promote a team's commitment to continuous improvement. As teams and teachers work to implement lessons focused on proficiency, they will undoubtedly recognize ways that can better support student achievement. In paying closer attention to students' developing proficiency, teams will begin to have more focused and intentional conversations about students who are struggling and how to help them more directly.

Likewise, they will begin to have richer, collaborative discussions focused on how to support students who are approaching proficiency, how to advance students who are beginning to demonstrate proficiency, and how to help support students who are beginning to demonstrate mastery learning.

Key Takeaways From Chapter 6

Review these key points with your team to reinforce the concepts from this chapter.

1. Promote feedback as a conversation with students, not as a comment that might sound like a grade. The purpose of proficiency-based instruction is to promote discussion about learning and how to continuously improve.

2. Include summative evaluations earlier in the learning process in ways that help solidify a foundation for learning and to ensure assessments are not designed as high-stakes experiences for students. Assessments should promote growth and awareness.

3. One element of proficiency-based instruction is to cultivate learning stamina. We want to create learners who understand the value of continuous improvement and perseverance.

4. Proficiency-based instructional practices should build learning confidence. Construct feedback practices that encourage the learning process.

5. In a lesson, create learning tension, which pushes students to new levels. The purpose of a lesson should be to help students develop. Adding an appropriate amount of tension can help the learner increase his or her developing strengths.

6. Remember, proficiency-based instruction works against the traditional one-size-fits-all model of lesson planning. Personalize the learning.

7. Proficiency-based instruction should extend the learning for all students—even the high flyers. Be sure to prepare your lessons so you can extend learning for students who have already mastered the content.

Stop, Think, Reflect

With your team, reflect on the following two questions to continue with the collaborative process for change.

1. In what ways is your team collaborating to address the seven takeaways from this chapter so you are collaborating for continuous improvement?

2. Return to your ongoing discussions about intervention practices. In what ways are interventions helping all students to achieve? Are the interventions working as planned, or should your team make other supports available for students?

chapter 7

Proficiency-Based Lessons in the Classroom

This chapter includes specific examples of how the proficiency-based lesson (created from the instructional diamond template) works in the real world of the classroom.

The following story has been modified for readability but is based on an actual proficiency-based lesson. In this example, a teacher is trying out a proficiency-based lesson for the first time. The lesson focuses on proficiency and efficacy development through individual, small-group, and whole-class engagement. As your read, see if you can spot where each segment fits into the instructional diamond template, as shown in figure 7.1.

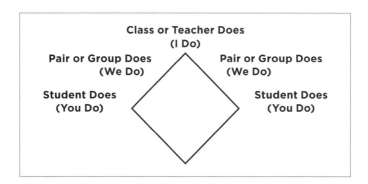

Figure 7.1: Instructional diamond lesson plan—Student-first model.

The Story of Ms. Ortiz's Class

It is a fall day in a government class in a local high school. The teacher, Ms. Ortiz, opens the class with a general question about what it means to be patriotic. After the students individually ponder the question and engage in thoughtful small-group dialogue, they personally reflect on what *patriotic* means to them, their school, their families, and their country.

Ms. Ortiz then calls on groups to share bits of their conversations. She adds this information to a class-created definition of what it means to be *patriotic*. After this initial activity, she directs students to engage in an activity where they will intentionally develop the following competency: *recognizing content and concepts in varying contexts with no support.*

The students are a little apprehensive at first, as this seems very difficult. It is not like anything they have ever done. They are used to answering questions about government terms and concepts, but they have always had support, such as word banks and vocabulary lists. This is the first time they have actually learned government through competency development instead of content acquisition.

Ms. Ortiz starts the activity, which is a brief formative assessment of multiple-choice questions, which students complete while staying in their groups. She reminds students that in order to be fully competent, they must be able to *recognize government content and concepts in varying contexts with no support.*

The students, who are used to Ms. Ortiz leading them step by step through the learning, proceed directly into the full application of competency from the beginning. The risk of failure is now extremely high. Ms. Ortiz, however, has created a highly formative environment that promotes failure in safe and secure ways. Her presence gives the students the confidence that they can learn by failing.

Students begin the activity by trying to answer the questions without the aid of a word bank, notes, book, or even the teacher. They have never been introduced to these words, nor have they had any context provided prior to this activity; they are simply asked to try.

As Ms. Ortiz walks around the room, students engage in conversation within their groups centered on the competency. She reminds the students that at any point they can look at their notes, books, or packets but then quickly adds that in order to be considered fully competent, they cannot do so.

Most students continue to work with their groups without any support and embrace the failure. They talk about the questions they do not know the answers to, and they openly discuss why they do not know those answers, what the words might mean, or what the context might be implying. Other students are making the tough choice, whether to peek at the word bank or open a page of their notes, but are then pausing because they know to be fully confident in their competence, they shouldn't look at the notes. She pauses the class for a few moments and clarifies some key terms and concepts by sharing some student responses from prior years.

In a few moments, students seem to realize that they do not need the word bank to complete the activity; thus, they become more confident about their learning because they accomplished it at the expected competency level. There seems to be a sort of gravitational pull toward the outlined competency, meaning it feels as if every conversation, word, action, and engagement directly relates to the competency level.

Groups then continue to refine their work with a more self-guided approach. Ms. Ortiz seems to be less of a central figure in the class, and students begin to act more self-reliant.

Ms. Ortiz then ends the class with a simple question: "Do you feel that you can recognize concepts and content in varying contexts without any support?" Some students state emphatically that they are more confident in their competency and that it will lead to success. Some state they are still unsure of where their competency is and where it will ultimately lead them. Others have a realistic understanding of what their competency is in the course. The ones who leave with full confidence in their competency are the ones who leave with the most important skill we can instill in our students— efficacy. This should be the goal of all instruction.

This story is an example of how a teacher, through instruction, can develop the singular trait of efficacy and highlights how to organize instruction in a new manner that can promote efficacy through competency, which not only will help students with their learning but also allow them to create their own learning and success as they go through life.

More examples like Ms. Ortiz's lesson are highlighted in the next chapter and can act as a guide on what a proficiency-based lesson should or could look like. As you review the following examples, notice how the proficiency-based lesson engages students in the proficiency experience earlier than in a traditional lesson. Also, notice that the proficiency-based lesson creates more time for reflection, reperformance, and conversation than a traditional lesson. And finally, notice how the proficiency-based lesson design creates more personal agency than a traditional lesson.

Proficiency-Based Lesson-Planning Templates

At Adlai E. Stevenson High School in Lincolnshire, Illinois, teachers use the proficiency-based lesson-planning template, or instructional diamond, in figure 7.2 (page 120) to change their traditional lessons to proficiency-based lessons.

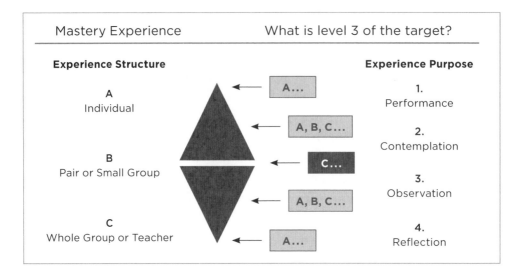

Figure 7.2: Diamond lesson-plan template: Tool for planning a proficiency-based lesson.

To use the template, a teacher simply chooses a structure from the left and combines it with a purpose on the right. For example, a teacher might pick an A2 activity (individual, contemplation) or a C3 activity (whole group, observation).

After this, the teacher simply places these activities into the instructional diamond lesson-planning template to create a proficiency-based lesson. See the example in figure 7.3.

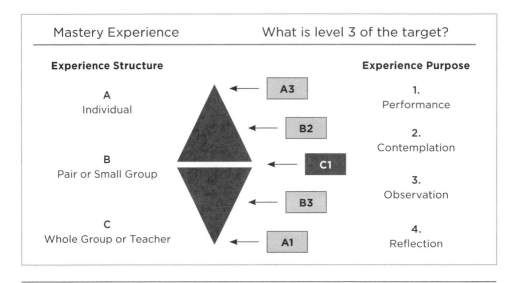

Figure 7.3: Example proficiency-based lesson using the instructional diamond template.

Because this process might be hard to visualize, we have provided two before-and-after lesson-plan examples using the instructional diamond, as shown in figure 7.4 and figure 7.5 (page 122). In these figures, the middle column shows a traditional lesson plan, and the right column shows a proficiency-based lesson plan. As you review these figures, note that the parts students *do* appear much earlier in the proficiency-based lesson plan than in the traditional one.

Learning Target: Accurately analyze a graph.		
Time	**Traditional Lesson Plan**	**Proficiency-Based Lesson Plan**
9:00–9:20 a.m.	Activate prior knowledge.	Introduce how to accurately analyze a graph.
9:20–9:30 a.m.	Introduce new terms and content.	Students complete graphing analysis problems.
9:30–9:40 a.m.	Assign short reading and provide sample graphs.	Assign short reading and provide sample graphs.
9:40–9:50 a.m.	Introduce how to analyze a graphing target.	Students complete graphing analysis problems.
9:50–10:10 a.m.	Students complete graphing analysis problems.	Students complete exit slip reflections on proficiency using the target.
10:10–10:15 a.m.	Students complete exit slip reflections on what terms they didn't know.	In our experience, proficiency-based lessons expedite learning and development. We have consistently found more time that can be repurposed to meet student learning needs.

Figure 7.4: Comparison of a traditional lesson plan with a proficiency-based lesson plan—Target: *Accurately analyze a graph.*

In the traditional lesson, students don't explore proficiency with the target until the very end of the lesson. However, in the proficiency-based lesson, students explore proficiency immediately and then the learning for the rest of the lesson relates to that moment.

Also, the reflection at the end of each lesson is much different. The traditional lesson offers just rote practice of supporting content, but the proficiency-based lesson asks students whether they feel their work is proficient. This type of reflection increases one's ability to self-appraise, thus developing a more accurate perception of their proficiency.

Figure 7.5 compares a traditional and proficiency-based lesson plan on giving a presentation.

Learning Target: Give a presentation.		
Time	**Traditional Lesson Plan**	**Proficiency-Based Lesson Plan**
9:00–9:20 a.m.	Students write the definitions of terms and concepts needed for the speech. Students brainstorm ways to present a speech for a specific topic.	Give students terms and definitions needed for the speech. In pairs, students present a claim and listen to comments about their speeches.
9:20–9:30 a.m.	Students share a list of ideas for speaking about this topic with partners.	Students share feedback with partners.
9:30–9:40 a.m.	Students analyze sample speeches against a rubric.	Students share feedback from partners with the class. They think about the feedback and decide on how to improve their next performance. Model a good speech for students. Students then revise their speeches based on their observations.
9:40–9:50 a.m.	Students share their rubric scores with the class and then engage in a discussion.	Small student groups present their revised speeches to each other.
9:50–10:10 a.m.	Model a good speech for students.	Students individually record themselves presenting.
10:10–10:15 a.m.	Small groups discuss what makes that a good speech.	Student review their own presentations and provide feedback.
10:15–10:30 a.m.	Students reflect on what they will work on to improve their speeches.	

Figure 7.5: Comparison of a traditional lesson plan with a proficiency-based lesson plan—Target: *Give a presentation.*

In the traditional lesson, students review models of presentations and learn essential components of presenting *before* they present. However, in the proficiency-based lesson, they begin presenting almost immediately and learn about the essential components *while* they are engaged in the act of presenting.

In both of these examples the *student does* portion of the learning is near or at the beginning of the lesson. This is essential for increasing authenticity and relevance to learning, as students can use this experience to connect new ideas throughout the lesson.

Also, notice that the proficiency-based lesson is shorter. Typically, when students are using their own work to learn, learning takes hold faster (Carey, 2014). Thus there is less need to revisit and relearn aspects of the content or skill. When teachers implement proficiency-based lessons, they usually find that they can get through the learning quicker, because they put students into proficiency experiences earlier. They get to the point of the learning quicker and students retain the lesson material faster. As a result, teachers have more time to extend learning or reflect. What teacher doesn't want more time in their lessons for deeper exploration of the material?

The reproducible "Instructional Diamond Lesson-Planning Template" (page 125) provides guidance on how to create proficiency-based lessons. This template is a chart form of the instructional diamond. Teachers can use this template to fully describe the activity executed at each segment.

Teachers should create and deliver lessons that allow students to experience the natural fluctuations in their learning and promote self-regulation and self-initiation. The ultimate goal of instruction should be to help students successfully learn how to create competency themselves. In the next chapter, we provide stories about how some teachers worked through this idea and successfully implemented proficiency-based instruction in their classes.

Key Takeaways From Chapter 7

Review these key points with your team to reinforce the concepts from this chapter.

1. Take the time to compare and contrast lessons. Identify how each lesson promotes proficiency, and consider ways you can improve the lessons to attend to every student.

2. Pay close attention to how the lessons allow for formative development and strong, influential feedback. Your role as the teacher is to constantly and immediately coach the developing growth of every student.

Stop, Think, Reflect

With your team, reflect on the following two questions to continue with the collaborative process for change.

1. How can you make time to observe other teachers' classrooms during the process of building proficiency-based instructional changes? Peer observations can provide the support you need when making improvements. Likewise, you can identify insights about necessary changes in order to help student achievement.

2. What does excellent teaching look like in a well-designed lesson? At what points in the lesson is evidence of student learning and growth made visible? In what ways does this evidence of student learning promote instructional insights?

Instructional Diamond Lesson-Planning Template

Lesson Purpose:

Learning Target:

Time Allotted

Planned Activities

Individual students

Pairs or small groups

Teacher facilitated

Pairs or small groups

Individual students

chapter 8

Discipline-Specific Examples of Proficiency-Based Instruction

The challenge of proficiency-based instruction is that it can be difficult to organize and implement. Teachers usually prepare instructional segments from a task perspective, which make them easy to build and manage. However, teachers must prepare proficiency-based instructional segments from a mastery perspective. Even after reading this book, it may be challenging to visualize how to implement proficiency-based instruction.

Our goal is for students to spend more time in *proficiency development*. In order to build proficiency, students must spend a majority of their time in proficiency development (develop) experiences rather than proficiency preparation (deliver) experiences or proficiency evaluation (determine) experiences. Figure 8.1 shows how a teacher should break down a proficiency-based lesson into instructional segments.

In a proficiency-based grading model, in which proficiency-based instruction works best, teachers tend to consider assessment and instruction as the same thing. In other words, teachers consider every moment in their class as valuable time to develop proficiency. As stated in earlier chapters, in order to do this effectively, teachers should not see their classroom as just a place for instruction and assessment, or see their assessments as simply formative or summative. It is important to organize all events that occur in the classroom into three types of events: deliver, develop, and determine. Figure 8.1 shows what percentage of any given lesson teachers should assign to each event.

Deliver	Develop	Determine
15 percent	80 percent	5 percent

Figure 8.1: Typical proficiency-based lesson-plan time allocation.

A traditional lesson typically goes something like this: instruction, quiz, more instruction, then another quiz, project, and finally a review day and a test. If we labeled each aspect of this sequence with *deliver*, *develop*, and *determine*, we would see the following: instruction and review day would be mostly deliver events, quizzes and the project would be develop events, and the test would be a determine event. See figure 8.2.

Figure 8.2: Traditional lesson plan.

While this structure may be efficient, it doesn't create nearly enough proficiency experience segments. Let's look at a conversation we recently had with one of our mathematics teachers at Stevenson High School in order to illustrate how to change a traditional lesson plan to a proficiency-based lesson plan.

A Mathematics Story of Proficiency-Based Instruction

The concept of proficiency-based instruction was problematic for one of our mathematics teachers. She was attempting to make the change from traditional to proficiency-based instruction and noticed something was not working. The scores on quizzes were not aligning with the scores on the summative exam. Early indications of student learning (quizzes) suggested that the students were proficient, but the summative results suggested that they were not. When this happens, it may leave teachers scrambling to review and plug gaps in students' learning, and students could grow apathetic, suddenly realizing they may not have it down like they thought.

For example, the two proficiency development moments (formative quizzes) showed that students were proficient, while the evaluation moment (summative exam) showed that students were still developing foundational skills. Knowing that the answer would be in her response to the following question, we asked her, "Where is your mastery experience?" We were asking her to look at what she wrote in in the final section of her lesson-plan template (test pulling it all together). See figure 8.3.

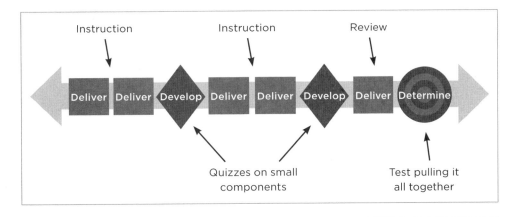

Figure 8.3: Traditional lesson or unit plan.

She answered that the mastery experience was in the determine event where the test was pulling it all together. See figure 8.4.

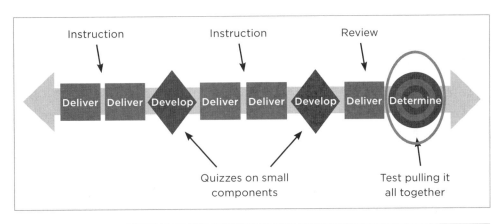

Figure 8.4: Traditional lesson or unit plan with identified mastery experience.

Before we proceed to the rest of our conversation, it's important to remember that deliver assessments are not proficiency experiences; they *prepare* students to begin to develop proficiency. It is similar to getting situated with all your hiking gear, maps, and park information before you begin a hiking trip. The deliver event would be packing your backpack, mapping your route, and consulting park rangers about the geography. The develop event would be the hike itself, as you reflect on your experience while it is happening. Did you bring the right equipment? Is the route the most efficient? How is your physical status? Finally, the determining event would be when you are done hiking and judge the experience. What is your hiking ability? Was it the experience you thought it would be? Are you a good hiker?

Proficiency experiences are when the teacher either develops or determines student proficiency, not when the teacher is preparing students to develop proficiency (deliver). See figure 8.5.

Deliver	Develop	Determine
Nonproficiency experiences (preparation)	Proficiency experiences (no stakes)	Proficiency experiences (high stakes)

Figure 8.5: Description of each assessment experience.

In this figure, it's important to understand not only the *purpose* of each experience but also the level of learning consequence that correlates it. The deliver experience should be *no stakes*, meaning it does not affect the final grade. The develop experience should mirror the determine experience, but it should be *no stakes* as well. Determine experiences should be *high stakes*, meaning that teachers use the evidence to calculate the final grade. Remember, in proficiency-based instruction, determine experiences don't only come at the end of a lesson or unit. They should be spread throughout the lesson or unit intermittently among the develop and deliver experiences.

Continuing our conversation, we asked the teacher, "Are your quizzes the same mastery experience as the determining assessment?" After some review, we deduced that the proficiency development experiences were actually deliver events, as shown in the following traditional lesson time line (see figure 8.6).

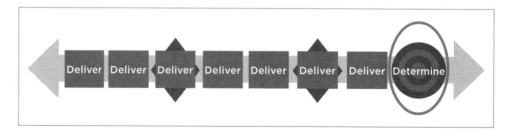

Figure 8.6: Traditional lesson or unit plan: Are your *develop* events actually *deliver* events?

What this teacher needed to do was *stretch* for a mastery experience earlier in the lesson. See figure 8.7.

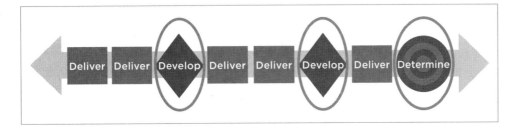

Figure 8.7: Ensuring that *develop* events are simulations of the *determine* event.

In proficiency-based instruction, you can take these three types of events—deliver, develop, and determine—and place them in any order and with any event you choose.

Remember, the goal of proficiency-based instruction is to collect as much evidence as you can to determine if a student is proficient in your expectations. There is no linear time-line template that you need to follow for this to happen.

The following two examples (see figure 8.8) are ways in which a teacher might structure a proficiency-based lesson or unit. These examples can apply to a segment of a lesson, a full lesson, or a full unit. It all depends on the course, grade level, or content area.

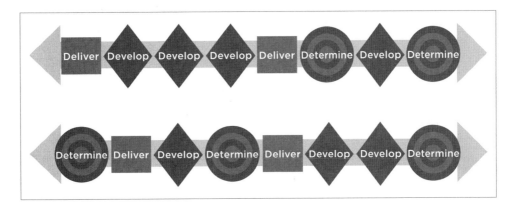

Figure 8.8: Mix and match: Using *deliver*, *develop*, and *determine* events to plan a proficiency-based lesson or unit.

A Social Studies Story of Proficiency-Based Instruction

A social studies teacher once asked us how to make his current lesson more proficiency based. He presented us with the following lesson plan. See figure 8.9 (page 132).

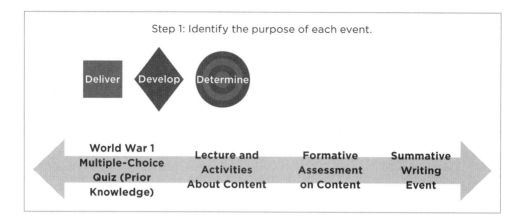

Figure 8.9: Step 1 in creating proficiency-based lessons.

We first asked him to identify each part of his lesson—deliver, develop, or determine. Then we asked him to label the mastery experience. Figure 8.10 shows his answer.

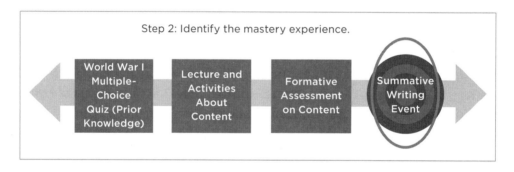

Figure 8.10: Step 2 in creating proficiency-based lessons.

We realized that there were no proficiency development moments, which are essential to developing proficiency and providing the teacher with enough evidence to judge student learning. Our suggestion was to insert moments of proficiency development, as shown in figure 8.11.

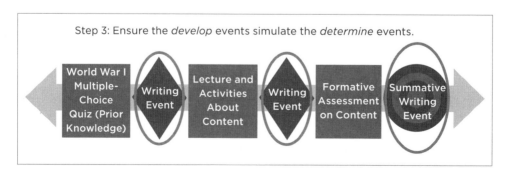

Figure 8.11: Step 3 in creating proficiency-based lessons.

Note there are two instances that align with the ultimate mastery experience (summative writing event): these writing events are proficiency development experiences. The teacher now has a better setup for the lesson to ensure students develop proficiency; all he had to do was add in a few moments of learning that align with the mastery experience.

The tool in figure 8.12 can help teachers with this process. You can find a reproducible version of this figure on page 135.

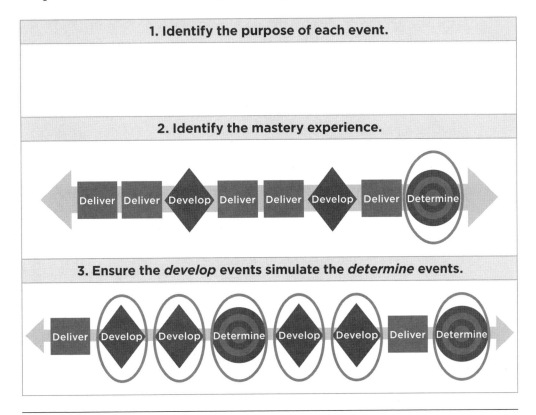

Figure 8.12: Laying out a proficiency-based lesson or unit.

As discussed in this chapter, instruction should mirror assessment and vice versa. This means that instruction is more simulation of the assessments than practice of the knowledge bits and skill components needed to perform the assessment. While the bits and components are necessary, students should learn them while engaged in the simulation, not prior. To do this, teachers must consider which aspects of their instruction simulate the proficiency experience on the exams or where they might have an opportunity to add a simulation event. This is not easy to do. This is why we offer the instructional diamond template as a guide. However, teachers still need to approach their instruction as assessment, ultimately viewing every moment in their classroom as a way to gather viable evidence of student proficiency.

Key Takeaways From Chapter 8

Review these key points with your team to reinforce the concepts from this chapter.

1. Every discipline is different and should be considered differently when designing proficiency-based instruction. Consider methods for assessing students effectively—what will engage students and what types of assessment practices promote a culture of learning.

2. As your team builds a bank of lessons, take the time to review and reflect on the structure of the lesson and the ways the lesson is promoting a proficiency-based classroom environment. Compare and contrast lessons and examine their value to student growth.

Stop, Think, Reflect

With your team, reflect on the following two questions to continue with the collaborative process for change.

1. Consider your team's focus and discipline. In what ways can you connect an approach to proficiency-based instruction to your learning discipline so assessment and learning are naturally integrated and not viewed as separate?

2. Again, focus on interventions. Does your team's discipline approach intervention strategies in ways that are innovative and supportive to student growth? How can you create intervention strategies that respond more immediately to student development so you can support students more effectively?

Proficiency-Based Instruction Planning Tool

1. Identify the purpose of each event.

2. Identify the mastery experience.

3. Ensure the *develop* events simulate the *determine* events.

References and Resources

Adair-Hauck, B., Glisan, E. W., & Troyan, F. J. (2013). *Implementing integrated performance assessment*. Alexandria, VA: American Council on the Teaching of Foreign Languages.

Ainsworth, L., & Viegut, D. (2006). *Common formative assessments: How to connect standards-based instruction and assessment*. Thousand Oaks, CA: Corwin Press.

Amabile, T. M. (1983). *The social psychology of creativity*. New York: Springer-Verlag.

Bandura, A. (1997). *Self-efficacy: The exercise of control*. New York: Freeman.

Bandura, A. (1982). The self and mechanisms of agency. In J. Suls (Ed.), *Psychological perspectives on the self* (Vol. 1, pp. 3–39). Hillsdale, NJ: Erlbaum.

Barnes, M. (2015). *Assessment 3.0: Throw out your grade book and inspire learning*. Thousand Oaks, CA: Corwin Press.

Barton, L. G. (1994). *Quick flip questions for critical thinking*. Greenwood Village, CO: Edupress.

Black, P. J., & Wiliam, D. (1998). *Inside the black box: Raising standards through classroom assessment* (1st ed.). London: King's College London School of Education.

Brimi, H. M. (2011, November). Reliability of grading high school work in English. *Practical Assessment, Research and Evaluation, 16*(17), 1–12.

Brookhart, S. M. (2017). *How to give effective feedback to your students* (2nd ed.). Alexandria, VA: Association for Supervision and Curriculum Development.

Brown, P. C., Roediger, H. L., & McDaniel, M. A. (2014). *Make it stick: The science of successful learning*. Cambridge, MA: Belknap Press of Harvard University Press.

Buehl, D. (2011). *Developing readers in the academic disciplines*. Newark, DE: International Reading Association.

Buffum, A., Mattos, M., & Weber, C. (2012). *Simplifying response to intervention: Four essential guiding principles*. Bloomington, IN: Solution Tree Press.

Burke, K. (1994). *The mindful school: How to assess authentic learning* (rev. ed.). Arlington Heights, IL: IRI/SkyLight.

Cardwell, M. E. (2011). *Patterns of relationships between teacher engagement and student engagement* (Doctoral dissertation). St. John Fisher College, Rochester, NY.

Carey, B. (2014). *How we learn: The surprising truth about when, where, and why it happens*. New York: Random House.

Chappuis, J. (2009). *Seven strategies of assessment for learning*. Portland, OR: Educational Testing Service.

Collins, J. (2001). *Good to great: Why some companies make the leap . . . and others don't*. New York: HarperCollins.

Csikszentmihalyi, M. (1990). *Flow: The psychology of optimal experience*. New York: Harper & Row.

Danielson, C. (2007). *Enhancing professional practice: A framework for teaching* (2nd ed.). Alexandria, VA: Association for Supervision and Curriculum Development.

Danielson, C. (2009). *Implementing the framework for teaching in enhancing professional practice*. Alexandria, VA: Association for Supervision and Curriculum Development.

Danielson, C. (2014). *The framework for teaching evaluation instrument* (2013 ed.). Princeton, NJ: Danielson Group. Accessed at www.danielsongroup.org /framework on January 5, 2019.

Dueck, M. (2014). *Grading smarter, not harder: Assessment strategies that motivate kids and help them learn*. Alexandria, VA: Association for Supervision and Curriculum Development.

Elbaum, D. (2015, May). The A.C.T. explorer reading model: Combining formative assessment and reading strategies. *The Assessor, 4*.

Elder, D. (2012). *Standard based teaching: A classroom guide*. Scotts Valley, CA: CreateSpace.

Flower, L. (1981). *Problem-solving strategies for writing*. New York: Harcourt Brace Jovanovich.

Gobble, T., Onuscheck, M., Reibel, A. R., & Twadell, E. (2016). *Proficiency-based assessment: Process, not product*. Bloomington, IN: Solution Tree Press.

Gobble, T., Onuscheck, M., Reibel, A. R., & Twadell, E. (2017). *Pathways to proficiency: Implementing evidence-based grading*. Bloomington, IN: Solution Tree Press.

Gonzalez, J. (2014). Know your terms: Anticipatory set. *Cult of Pedagogy.* Accessed at www.cultofpedagogy.com/anticipatory-set on December 12, 2018.

Gregory, K., Cameron, C., & Davies, A. (2011). *Self-assessment and goal setting* (2nd ed.). Bloomington, IN: Solution Tree Press.

Guo, K. (2015, February 28). What happens when students rent learning? *Statesman.* Accessed at www.statesmanshs.org/1055/features/what-happens-when -students-rent-learning on January 13, 2016.

Guskey, T. R. (2015). *On your mark: Challenging the conventions of grading and reporting.* Bloomington, IN: Solution Tree Press.

Guskey, T. R., & Bailey, J. M. (2001). *Developing grading and reporting systems for student learning.* Thousand Oaks, CA: Corwin Press.

Guskey, T. R., & Jung, L. (2013). *Answers to essential questions about standards, assessments, grading, and reporting.* Thousand Oaks, CA: Corwin Press.

Hattie, J. (2012). *Visible learning for teachers: Maximizing impact on learning.* London: Routledge.

Hattie, J., & Yates, G. C. R. (2014). *Visible learning and the science of how we learn.* London: Routledge.

Heflebower, T., Hoegh, J. K., & Warrick, P. (2014). *A school leader's guide to standards-based grading.* Bloomington, IN: Marzano Research.

Hunter, M. (1982). *Mastery teaching: Increasing instructional effectiveness in elementary and secondary schools, colleges, and universities.* Thousand Oaks, CA: Corwin Press.

Jain, D., & Reibel, A. (2018, May). Creating competence in the classroom. *The Assessor, 5,* 16–17.

Kendall, J. S., & Marzano, R. J. (1997). *Content knowledge: A compendium of standards and benchmarks for K–12 education* (2nd ed.). Aurora, CO: McREL.

Kohn, A. (2006). *The homework myth: Why our kids get too much of a bad thing.* Cambridge, MA: Da Capo Life Long.

Learning. (n.d.). In *Merriam-Webster's online dictionary.* Accessed at www.merriam -webster.com/dictionary/learning on March 28, 2019.

Lipton, L., & Wellman, B. (2011). *Groups at work: Strategies and structures for professional learning.* Charlotte, VT: MiraVia.

Marzano, R. J. (2003). *What works in schools: Translating research into action.* Alexandria, VA: Association for Supervision and Curriculum Development.

Marzano, R. J. (2006). *Classroom assessment and grading that work.* Alexandria, VA: Association for Supervision and Curriculum Development.

Marzano, R. J. (2009). *Designing and teaching learning goals and objectives.* Bloomington, IN: Marzano Research.

McTighe, J., & Ferrara, S. (1998). *Assessing learning in the classroom.* Washington, DC: National Education Association.

Moss, C. M., & Brookhart, S. M. (2012). *Learning targets: Helping students aim for understanding in today's lesson.* Alexandria, VA: Association for Supervision and Curriculum Development.

National Governors Association Center for Best Practices & Council of Chief State School Officers. (2010a). *Common Core State Standards for English language arts and literacy in history/social studies, science, and technical subjects.* Washington, DC: Authors. Accessed at www.corestandards.org/assets /CCSSI_ELA%20Standards.pdf on December 13, 2018.

National Governors Association Center for Best Practices & Council of Chief State School Officers. (2010b). *Common Core State Standards for mathematics.* Washington, DC: Authors. Accessed at www.corestandards.org/assets /CCSSI_Math%20Standards.pdf on December 13, 2018.

O'Connor, K. (2007). *A repair kit for grading: 15 fixes for broken grades.* Portland, OR: Educational Testing Service.

O'Connor, K. (2009). *How to grade for learning, K–12* (3rd ed.). Thousand Oaks, CA: Corwin Press.

O'Connor, K. (2011). *A repair kit for grading: 15 fixes for broken grades* (2nd ed.). Boston: Pearson.

Reeves, D. (2006). *The learning leader: How to focus school improvement for better results.* Alexandria, VA: Association for Supervision and Curriculum Development.

Reeves, D. (2008). Leading to change / effective grading practices. *Educational Leadership, 65*(5), 85–87.

Reeves, D. (2011). *Elements of grading: A guide to effective practice.* Bloomington, IN: Solution Tree Press.

Reibel, A. (2018a, May). Personal efficacy in education. *The Assessor, 5,* 19–20.

Reibel, A. (2018b, May). Three purposes of assessment: Deliver, develop, determine. *The Assessor, 5,* 14–15.

Ripley, A. (2013). *The smartest kids in the world: And how they got that way.* New York: Simon & Schuster.

Ritchhart, R., Church, M., & Morrison, K. (2011). *Making thinking visible: How to promote engagement, understanding, and independence for all learners.* San Francisco: Jossey-Bass.

Sandrock, P. (2011, December 8). *Designing backwards: From performance assessments to units of instruction.* Lecture conducted at the American Council on the Teaching of Foreign Languages, Lincolnshire, IL.

Savage, S. L. (2012). *The flaw of averages: Why we underestimate risk in the face of uncertainty.* Hoboken, NJ: Wiley.

Schoemaker, P. J. H. (2011). *Brilliant mistakes: Finding success on the far side of failure* [E-reader version]. Philadelphia: Wharton Digital Press.

Sperling, D. (1993). What's worth an "A"?: Setting standards together. *Educational Leadership, 50*(5), 73–75.

Starch, D., & Elliott, E. C. (1912). Reliability of the grading of high-school work in English. *School Review, 20*(7), 442–457.

Stiggins, R. (2006). Assessment *for* learning: A key to motivation and achievement. *EDge, 2*(2), 3–19.

Stiggins, R., Arter, J. A., Chappuis, J., & Chappuis, S. (2004). *Classroom assessment for student learning: Doing it right—using it well.* Portland, OR: Assessment Training Institute.

Stiggins, R., & Chappuis, J. (2008). Enhancing student learning. *District Administration, 44*(1), 42–44.

Terada, Y. (2017). How metacognition boosts learning. *Edutopia.* Accessed at www.edutopia.org/article/how-metacognition-boosts-learning on January 13, 2018.

Toffler, A. (1970). *Future shock.* New York: Random House.

Tovani, C. (2012). Feedback is a two-way street. *Educational Leadership, 70*(1), 48–51.

University of Illinois at Urbana–Champaign. (n.d.). *Illinois youth survey: Survey results.* Accessed at https://iys.cprd.illinois.edu/results on January 14, 2016.

Vatterott, C. (2009). *Rethinking homework: Best practices that support diverse needs.* Alexandria, VA: Association for Supervision and Curriculum Development.

Vatterott, C. (2015). *Rethinking grading: Meaningful assessment for standards-based learning.* Alexandria, VA: Association for Supervision and Curriculum Development.

Wiggins, G. (1996). Honesty and fairness: Toward better grading and reporting. In T. R. Guskey (Ed.), *Communicating student learning: The ASCD yearbook* (pp. 141–176). Alexandria, VA: Association for Supervision and Curriculum Development.

Wiggins, G. (2010, May 22). *Feedback: How learning occurs* [Blog post]. Accessed at www.authenticeducation.org/bigideas/article.lasso?artid=61 on June 20, 2015.

Wiggins, G., & McTighe, J. (2005). *Understanding by design* (Expanded 2nd ed.). Alexandria, VA: Association for Supervision and Curriculum Development.

Wiliam, D. (2011). *Embedded formative assessment.* Bloomington, IN: Solution Tree Press.

Willis, S. (1993). Are letter grades obsolete? *Education Update, 35*(7), 4–8.

Wormeli, R. (2014, November 12). *Standards-based assessment and grading.* Lecture conducted at the Illinois Association for Supervision and Curriculum Development's Curriculum 2020, DeKalb, IL.

Zizzo, J. (2015, November). Us vs. them: For whom is the feedback, anyway? *The Assessor,* 15.

Index

Proficiency-Based Assessment
Troy Gobble, Mark Onuscheck, Anthony R. Reibel, and Eric Twadell
With this resource, teachers will discover how to close the gaps between assessment, curriculum, and instruction by replacing outmoded assessment methods with proficiency-based assessments. Learn the essentials of proficiency-based assessment, and explore evidence-based strategies for successful implementation.
BKF631

Pathways to Proficiency
Troy Gobble, Mark Onuscheck, Anthony R. Reibel, and Eric Twadell
Adopt a new, more effective grading model for students. This book provides the pathway for implementing evidence-based grading practices in schools through a straightforward, five-phase creative model. Readers will follow a hypothetical curriculum team's challenging journey through each phase of this process.
BKF682

Proficiency-Based Grading in the Content Areas
Edited by Anthony R. Reibel and Eric Twadell
No matter the content area, evidence-based grading puts student growth at the heart of the classroom. Designed for teachers and administrators of grades 6–12, *Proficiency-Based Grading in the Content Areas* details how to effectively implement evidence-based grading and maintain its effectiveness over time.
BKF837

The New Art and Science of Teaching
Robert J. Marzano
This title is a greatly expanded volume of the original *The Art and Science of Teaching*, offering a framework for substantive change based on Dr. Marzano's 50 years of education research. While the previous model focused on teacher outcomes, the new version places focus on student outcomes.
BKF776

Wait! Your professional development journey doesn't have to end with the last pages of this book.

We realize improving student learning doesn't happen overnight. And your school or district shouldn't be left to puzzle out all the details of this process alone.

No matter where you are on the journey, we're committed to helping you get to the next stage.

Take advantage of everything from **custom workshops** to **keynote presentations** and **interactive web and video conferencing**. We can even help you develop an action plan tailored to fit your specific needs.

Let's get the conversation started.

Call 888.763.9045 today.

solution-tree.com